# PLAY TO POTENTIAL

# ADVANCE PRAISE FOR THE BOOK

'Deepak builds on the wisdom distilled from more than a hundred iconic business leaders, academics and role models'—**Abhijit Bhaduri, author and personal branding coach**

'Deepak's new book lays out a powerful and new framework [of] FLAVOUR. Most of us chase success without thinking about the purpose of life. I love the fact that Deepak emphasizes the family context, our aspirations, how we create value, and invest in ourselves and deep relationships. The book should be read every year as we have to constantly rediscover and reaffirm our purpose towards leading a happy and meaningful life'—**Ashish Dhawan, founder and CEO, The Convergence Foundation**

'Deepak's *Play to Potential* podcast is a library of insights for unlocking potential across multiple disciplines—arts, business, sports and more. Through this book and his unique FLAVOUR model, he distils what it takes to lead a full life and play the long game'—**Atul Kasbekar, photographer and producer**

'Deepak is a student of journeys and transitions and is curious about how each one of us can be the best version of ourselves in a multidimensional sense. As a big fan of *ikigai*, I found that his book provides more relatable methods to process a real multidimensional life given the various pulls and pressures we face. And the frameworks are useful no matter which life stage one is in! Highly recommend and thank you, Deepak, for capturing these insights'—**Avnish Bajaj, co-founder and general partner, Z47 (formerly known as Matrix Partners India)**

'If you truly want to "play to potential", [then] this useful, practical and actionable guide offers clear insights on how to make a deeper connection with yourself and the wider world, so you can lead a fuller and more FLAVOUR-ful life. Highly recommended'—**Bharat Puri, managing director, Pidilite Industries Limited**

'In a world obsessed with external markers of success, *Play to Potential* arrives with a refreshing reminder: True fulfilment comes from within. Through a blend of insights from his podcast, coaching practice and personal journey, Deepak presents a compelling case for embracing our uniqueness and crafting a life that aligns with our deepest values'—**Daniel H. Pink, #1 *New York Times* bestselling author of *The Power of Regret***

'How can we stay grounded while chasing our professional and personal dreams? And, stay oriented to our inner selves while making the transitions we must? Deepak Jayaraman draws on his wide experiences as an executive coach and his *Play to Potential* podcast, to look beyond ikigai and provide an exciting new framework'—**Cyrus Vakil, former principal, Bombay International School**

'Deepak, through his coaching, has been instrumental in honing my life and leadership to be holistic and multidimensional. He now translates his years of practical coaching into an insightful playbook to help unleash your potential towards a well-meaning and harmonious life'—**Gaganjot Singh, president and managing director (Africa, India and the Middle East), Michelin**

'As I absorbed the true essence of Deepak's deep insights, I loved the way he talked about potential across every phase of life and for every kind of person—whether a student, homemaker, professional or retired person. For me, the book brought to life how I can look at my potential going forward'—**Govind Iyer, philanthropist and board member**

'*Play to Potential* is a compelling read for every person who wishes to walk through life thoughtfully. The author, Deepak Jayaraman, builds on his rich and diverse experiences to guide us through the many FLAVOURs of living a beautiful life that is well balanced, productive and fulfilling. This book is a must-read because it can transform the way you think about the years ahead of you'—**Harish Bhat, former brand custodian, Tata Sons, avid marketer and bestselling author**

'I have found Deepak to be a curious student of human potential. If you aspire to lead a multidimensional life, his book, filled with examples and stories, might show you the path'—**Harsh Mariwala, chairman, Marico Limited, philanthropist and author**

'I have witnessed Deepak's transformation over the last twenty-five years from being a thoughtful classmate at IIMA in 1997–99 to an affable colleague to a trusted adviser now. One thing about Deepak that stands out consistently through the years is his total dedication and sincerity about everything he takes up—be it learning to juggle, single sculling or running a successful podcast or becoming a sought-after coach. With his deep experience as an organization consultant and the stellar body of podcasts he has curated as key ingredients, his book will definitely add a positive FLAVOUR to our lives'—**Kaushika Madhavan, managing partner and country head, Kearney India**

'*Play to Potential* provides actionable insights for crafting a life of purpose and fulfilment. Grounded in Deepak's extensive consulting experience and podcast interviews with industry and academic leaders, *Play to Potential* goes beyond traditional frameworks like ikigai and offers a unique framework that transcends traditional career advice by emphasizing the interconnectedness of family, aspirations, value creation, self-investment and nurturing relationships. A must-read for anyone seeking to live a truly "FLAVOUR-ful" life'—**Kartik Hosanagar, John C. Hower Professor of Technology and Digital Business and professor of marketing at The Wharton School, University of Pennsylvania**

'DJ's book is a beacon of light for people seeking their path in an increasingly fragmented, noisy and cluttered world. Drawing from his own life experiences and the wisdom of his brilliant podcast *Play to Potential*, his potpourri of insights is simple and compelling—a must-read, especially for those navigating the roller coaster of midlife'—**Kavita Iyer, managing trustee, Singhal Iyer Family Foundation and co-founder, Young Artiste**

'*Play to Potential* draws on Deepak's immersive work with leaders from across domains, presenting actionable insights to build a full life. It is an accessible book, presented in a truly engaging way. I found it a valuable read, and plan to share it with [my] clients as well as my newly adult children!'—**Moomal Mehta, founder, Crossover Catalyst**

'Thoughtful, pragmatic and deeply insightful. This book is a gem. Highly recommended for anyone navigating a "what next" phase in their journey'—**Mrinalini Mirchandani, senior partner, McKinsey & Company**

'Richly researched, [this book is] absolutely interesting and insightful. At the same time, [it is] real and relatable, [something] that would trigger you "to take a pause", "to reflect", "to take steps to rediscover" and "to reform" yourself. Highly recommended'—**Navin Wadhwani, head of investment banking, J.P. Morgan**

'There are people who define roles and there are roles that define people. Deepak absolutely fits the former. Every time I meet Deepak, I walk away feeling enriched—a new idea to embrace, a new thinking hat to try or just a sense of calmness. DJ spends time reflecting deeply on topics—I have listened to many podcasts over the years, but his *Play to Potential* was truly exceptional.

'When DJ told me that he was writing a book, it felt like the right thing to do. We then had a lovely dinner together, during which he took me through the thinking of a FLAVOR-ful life to unlock my full potential. I was captivated. DJ has poured the right mix of thoughtfulness and a fair dose of love into bringing this book together. And what has come together is a reference text which will be a go-to place for many'—**Neeraj Aggarwal, chair, Asia Pacific, Boston Consulting Group**

'Deepak is one of the most introspective and thoughtful people I know. His book is a synthesis of the many conversations he has had [with people from all walks of life], and is a must-read!'—**Neeraj Sagar, founder, Wisdom Circle**

'I have known Deepak for more than a decade and his passion for making a difference to people's lives shines through. He has now authored a book, which provides a holistic framework for people to live a meaningful life. This framework is called "FLAVOUR" and is pragmatic and balanced. Definitely worth its weight in gold, highly recommended!'—**Niren Shah, managing director and head, Norwest India**

'Deepak is incredibly passionate about helping people holistically unlock their full potential cutting across personal and professional spheres. He's made a difference in several lives and continues on this mission through his latest book. In this book, Deepak lays out a model that builds on his unique insights as a coach to leaders in different contexts to help them play to their potential. It is not just a theoretical framework but a nuanced, practical perspective based on several conversations with respected leaders'—**Nishant Sharma, co-founder, Kedaara Capital**

'Few people have studied life's transitions as deeply as Deepak. He has wonderfully distilled wisdom from hundreds of incredibly successful people who have navigated their life's transitions beautifully. That makes this book a modern-day manual for how to live a wholesome life in an ever-changing world. Thank you for this incredible gift, Deepak'—**Papa CJ, stand-up comedian, executive coach and author**

'Deepak is masterful at creating a model of leadership that focuses on the entire human being, not just the professional. He taps into the wisdom he has gleaned from his *Play to Potential* podcast and marries it with his experiences as a coach to offer an innovative approach to unlocking our potential'—**Pramath Sinha, founder and trustee, Ashoka University, and founding dean, Indian School of Business**

'I have been engaging with Deepak Jayaraman, an accomplished leadership coach, over the last couple of years. He has been able to develop context and trust quickly, been a great sounding board in many difficult decisions and helped immensely in my leadership journey.

'This book emphasizes coherence across the elements of FLAVOUR and the importance of contextual familiarity. It opens the possibility of multiple paths, making it applicable to everyone from homemakers to entrepreneurs. In my journey, I've struggled with "how" more than "what", and this book provides a practical, powerful approach to start on the journey and finding that balance'—**Pranav Goel, co-founder, Porter**

'Deepak has inspired me, provoked me and always made me think differently. He does the same with this book. This book offers a compelling framework and meta-skills for rediscovering yourself and thinking hard about what really floats your boat in life. A timely reminder to not ignore the hidden metrics (family, self-awareness, relationships) for the visible ones (money, designation). A must-read, and more importantly, an opportunity to reflect as we rediscover the FLAVOUR in our lives'—**Puneet Chandok, president, Microsoft India and South Asia**

'If you are in your thirties or fifties and are unsure about how to extract the most happiness and fulfilment out of the rest of your life, please do yourself a favour and pick this book. You'll walk away with greater potential to play to your potential!'—**Raj Raghunathan, author of** *If You Are So Smart, Why Aren't You Happy?*

'Deepak has put together a guide that is simultaneously deeply thoughtful and immensely practical to helping midlife professionals play to their potential. He masterfully combines his own experiences and reflections, which he shares with humility and vulnerability, learnings from his prolific podcast that has featured accomplished individuals from across the globe as well as detailed journeys of six inspiring individuals who are bringing "FLAVOUR" to their lives. The book is presented as a combination of words, images and audio that makes for an instructive read for anyone interested in taking charge of their destiny and living a life filled with meaning and purpose'—**Rajiv Lochan, managing director and chief executive officer, Sundaram Finance Limited**

'Discovering and fulfilling our potential is a fundamental human need. However, way too often, it is viewed narrowly, and its pursuit [is] confined to our professional lives. Capturing the wisdom distilled from his rich experiences, Deepak's book beautifully shines the light on a much-needed holistic approach to realizing our greater potential as human beings'—**Rajiv Vij, life and executive coach, and author of *Inside-Out Leadership: 16 Radical Insights Successful Leaders Wish They Had Discovered***

'The book you truly need to navigate midlife turbulence'—**Rashmi Bansal, author of many bestselling books**

'Tired of the "achievement at all costs" mentality? In *Play to Potential*, Deepak shows you how to achieve success without sacrificing your well-being. Packed with insights from fascinating conversations with extraordinary leaders, you will learn to define your own "FLAVOUR" of success and lead a life that's both meaningful and impactful. Highly recommended'—**Ravi Venkatesan, social entrepreneur, business leader and writer**

'Deepak Jayaraman has established himself as a thoughtful and impactful coach to help professionals reach their full potential, through his individual context-based approach.

I am delighted that his new book *Play to Potential* will allow a larger audience to benefit from his ideas and unique perspective'—**Rishikesha Krishnan, director, IIM Bangalore**

'A handy guide for reflection and designing a balanced and fulfilling life. Deepak skilfully combines insights from leadership interviews, frameworks and tools, as well as relatable stories from his journey, making this an engaging read'—**Roopa Kudva, former managing director, CRISIL, and head, Omidyar Network, India**

'Deepak has adeptly combined his own lived experiences and those of others to give us a new way of thinking about how we live our fullest lives. *Play to Potential* is a must-read if you are reflecting on your own journey thus far and interested in making the most of the years ahead'—**Ritwik Bhattacharya, chief technology officer, Headspace**

'Deepak has played a pivotal role in my personal journey, embodying the essence of effective coaching and mentorship. His profound wisdom, strategic guidance and steadfast belief in my potential have been the bedrock of my growth.

'Deepak's book is an indispensable resource for anyone committed to living a balanced and purposeful life. It doesn't just encourage reflection; [but] it [also] provides a thoughtful and actionable road map for navigating the complexities of life with intention and grace. It challenges readers to deeply reflect on their core values, transform their regrets into learning experiences and draw inspiration from the lives of others to navigate life's pivotal transitions. For me, this book is not just a guide; it's a blueprint to lead a balanced and meaningful life'—**Sachinder Bhinder, managing director and chief executive officer, Aavas Financiers Ltd**

'No one I know thinks about human potential and achieving our potential in a holistic sense as much as Deepak does. Over the past decade, he has helped hundreds of people, through his practice and several thousands through his podcast, take the first steps to unlock their potential. I am glad he has chosen to distil his life's learnings on how we can play to our full potential through this book'—**Sajith Pai, investor, Blume Ventures**

'In the quest to live a purposeful, value-driven, successful and happy life, every professional mixes his own cauldron of elements to evolve "life's recipes"! Deepak has put together distilled wisdom from the learnings of over 100 professionals, entrepreneurs, men and women of substance in the *Play to Potential* podcast that gives insights on personal skills, forming perspectives, building interesting facets to your life and career and hopefully finding happiness. A must-read for the beginner in a career and the well-heeled ones to polish their framework'—**Suresh Narayanan, chairman and managing director, Nestlé India Limited**

'I have known Deepak since our days in high school, lived in the same dorm in college and worked together on our senior project, and it's amazing to see his transformation into what he is doing for leaders across the world now. I personally have gone through my own set of positive transformations at work and in my personal life, and I take a lot of inspiration from what's beautifully covered in this book'—**Umesh Subramanian, chief technology officer (CTO), Citadel, and ex-CTO, Goldman Sachs**

'Deepak is rare in the coaching profession in that he takes his own medicine. Within these pages you will find not just Deepak's perspective on others gleaned from many years working with top executives but also reflections from a life that has been shaped in the heat of facing up to himself, investing in his own development and building, as he would call it, a FLAVOUR-ful life. I would strongly recommend it'—**Vivek Vijay Khemka, partner, Egon Zehnder**

'Deepak brings enormous curiosity to understanding what helps individuals live their life to the fullest. From the personal, starting with family and ending with relationships, to the professional—creating space for what you love and many other dimensions—this book is full of FLAVOUR brought in from conversations with 100+ leaders across India and beyond. At the very least, this book can help you reflect and rebalance your life. At its best, it can help you truly realize your potential!'—**Venkat Krishnan, founder, GiveIndia, and philanthropy evangelizer**

'*Play to Potential* is a remarkable idea, executed brilliantly by Deepak, which centres the full potential of an individual, rather than fragmenting personal and professional achievements thereby hiding the "real" person'—**Vinita Bali, strategy adviser and independent director**

'A compelling journey into discovering what it takes to play to one's full potential! Deepak has skilfully woven together scholarly insights from 100+ experts with inspiring, real-life stories to create a bold, new FLAVOUR, with his uniquely authentic and thoughtful voice.

'When I allowed myself to be open and vulnerable and, at times uncomfortable, I found this book fascinating, deeply insightful, liberating, soul-stirring and fun! An invitation to each one of us to celebrate our uniqueness in our own context with a distinctive FLAVOUR. Highly recommended!'—**Vikas Srivastava, former area managing director, Johnson & Johnson**

'In a world, where everyone has the disposition to voice their learnings with a buzzy clickbait on LinkedIn, Deepak is that rare craftsman, who has truly distilled the wisdom that he has gathered from his lived experience on the back of a practitioner's knowledge and real-life work. What is special is that he has done so by challenging orthodoxy in this book. Most books on leadership and life offer a monotheistic framework of what "ideal" looks like. Like Swami Vivekananda, who could synthesize Hinduism's polytheistic framework from *isht devata* to Advaitic Vedanta and lay them like steps for the striving soul, Deepak has done that for a professional by tailoring and sharing examples of what ideal would like in the context of that person's life—that empathizes with their stage, need and moment and is, therefore, highly personalized for them'—**V.T. Bharadwaj, co-founder and general partner, A91 Partners**

# PLAY TO POTENTIAL

*Lead a full life, become the best you*

## DEEPAK JAYARAMAN

PENGUIN
BUSINESS

An imprint of Penguin Random House

PENGUIN BUSINESS

Penguin Business is an imprint of the Penguin Random House group of companies
whose addresses can be found at global.penguinrandomhouse.com

Published by Penguin Random House India Pvt. Ltd
4th Floor, Capital Tower 1, MG Road,
Gurugram 122 002, Haryana, India

First published in Penguin Business by Penguin Random House India 2024

Copyright © Deepak Jayaraman 2024

ISBN 9780670099986

Typeset in Adobe Caslon Pro by Manipal Technologies Limited, Manipal
Printed at Thomson Press India Ltd, New Delhi

www.penguin.co.in

# Contents

## SECTION C: AN APPROACH TO A FULL LIFE

# Why I Wrote This Book

## And Why You Might Find It of Value

It was 1 February 2016. I moved out from Egon Zehnder, an executive search firm, to set up my own leadership advisory and transitions practice. I was (still am) on a quest to understand how each one of us can play to our full potential as a human being. That led to my starting the *Play to Potential* podcast later in 2016, which put me on a learning journey to understand how accomplished practitioners (business leaders, sports(wo)men, artists etc.) and leading academics thought about the various elements of playing to our full potential.

Speaking to 100+ luminaries on the podcast, including Ivy League professors, Thinkers50 Coaching Legends, Padma Shri awardees and world champions helped me build a more nuanced understanding of the various dimensions

involved in playing to our full potential. My profession as
a coach and a sounding board to leaders also gave me an
intimate view of the trials and tribulations of individuals
seeking to unlock their potential.

When I juxtaposed these learnings with my journey,
three themes emerged from these reflections.

Firstly, life is a team sport, not a solo sport. The team
being family! This is particularly true in India, the culture
I am most familiar with. The more people I spoke to, it
seemed that there are many cultures in Asia, Latin America,
Africa and some parts of Europe where we play the sport
of life as a team, which is our family. Radius of what we
mean by family might vary across cultures but in most
cases, it includes parents, siblings, spouse and children.
While playing to our full potential is an individual pursuit,
it is something we embark on in the context of the families
we live in. I felt that the current literature wasn't giving
adequate attention to the family context.

Secondly, while life feels like a continuum, I noticed
that there are seasons which are often punctuated by clear
transitions—some that we make of our volition and some
that are imposed upon us. Losing my father to cancer in
2008 brought me from the US to India and catalyzed a
journey from management consulting to executive search.
The arrival of my second child got me to think harder
about the intensity with which I want to run my life and
got me to start my coaching practice. As I looked around,
I came to realize that playing to potential is as much about
navigating these life transitions thoughtfully as it is about

playing a season well across the long game of life. I noticed that a lot of the literature around speaks to you at a point in time but not across the seasons.

Thirdly, I came to realize that a north star cannot play the role of a torchlight. They serve different purposes. A lot of the literature I came across didn't quite account for the messiness of life. Very often, we need to work in jobs that we don't enjoy because we need the money to feed the family. Women often quit their jobs after maternity because they don't have the family support to take care of their children or because childcare is expensive. Passion and purpose, I discovered, are things that we figure out as we walk our path. They are not things that we clearly know upfront. Life, I have come to realize, is a lot messier than the way it is characterized. I found many books that romanticized the moon but none that spoke about navigating the craters in it.

Armed with the wisdom from the podcast, my coaching conversations and reflections from my journey, I offer a possible approach that is holistic, granular and can hopefully stay with us through the seasons of our life.

I sincerely hope that this book helps you navigate the pulls and pressures of life and gives you agency to take baby steps in unlocking your potential as a human being.

Mumbai, 19 August 2024

# Foreword

As a schoolboy, I was once forced to read a 1915 essay by the English philosopher G.K. Chesterton called 'The Fallacy of Success'. It begins as follows: 'There has appeared in our time a particular class of books and articles which I sincerely and solemnly think may be called the silliest ever known among men . . . These are books showing men how to succeed in everything; they are written by men who cannot even succeed in writing books.'

Deepak Jayaraman's book, *Play to Potential*, is the antithesis to all that Chesterton reviles. It is targeted at what DJ, as he is also fondly called, euphemistically calls Type-2 personalities. Those who, as he says, 'do not wish to go for professional success while sacrificing health, relationships and other pursuits that provide fulfilment and meaning. They are looking to unlock their full potential as human beings, especially through the pulls and pressures of midlife'.

The pulls and pressures of midlife or the messy midlife are rites of passage.

In our callow years most of us buy into the groupthink of 'success', especially as something that is by and large a zero-sum game. If somebody is successful, then somebody else, by the same definition, is a failure. Success guarantees happiness and failure unhappiness. But, if by the time you are in the middle of your life, you don't have at least a hazy sense that all that you have slogged for in your life doesn't really add up to much, you are either enlightened or have a lot of maturing to do.

When in Henry James' classic *The Ambassadors*, Mr Strether says, 'I with my back quite as bent, have never made anything. I am a perfectly equipped failure.' Miss Gostrey replies, 'Thank goodness you're a failure—it's why I distinguish you! Anything else today is too hideous. Look about you—look at the successes. Would you be one, on your honour?'

If sometimes, like most people, you feel like Mr Strether, then it's the first reason to read this book.

The second one, of course, is DJ himself.

DJ has been different from most of us. A product of IIT Madras and IIM Ahmedabad (IIMA), he must have been under social pressure to conform to the standard hierarchies of success. Yet as his classmate at IIMA, I already saw him discriminating between what the world saw as success and what he saw as happiness. He wanted to be in the supply chain of a company like Asian Paints. But the strict hierarchy of IIMA put tremendous pressure on high-graders like DJ to join management consulting. Ultimately, he conformed and chose consulting, but the fact that he even went through this angst meant his messy midlife (read maturing) started in his early twenties.

By his late thirties, when most of us hadn't entered our midlife crisis, DJ was comfortably out of it. He had figured out the FLAVOUR of life that suited him the most. Placing **F**amily first, creating space for things he **L**oves (he enjoys learning and playing the guitar), working towards his **A**spirations of doing more in the social sector, adding **V**alue as a coach and podcaster, seeing **O**pportunity in transitions as a space, investing in his health and having the time to cultivate **R**elationships that matter to him. When DJ walks into a room you cannot but notice in him a Buddha who hasn't fully forsaken the world. So, if at some point you want to be like DJ—contented, healthy, ever helpful, multidimensional and holistic across the various facets of life—then the book may give you some tips.

Since 2016, DJ has systematically interviewed over 100 people in his podcast *Play to Potential*. Many of the interviewees are successful, some worthy of emulation, but almost all of them are interesting. This unique primary research has given DJ a ringside view into ideas of success and potential. For instance, the book mentions a podcast episode with chess legend Viswanathan Anand in which he speaks about 'a unique dynamic that plays out around Move 40 in chess'. Anand says that when players cross move 40, they are often given a new block of time to play the next few moves. Anand speaks about how players (including him) often carry the stress of moves 37, 38, 39 and 40 into moves 41, which ends up being counterproductive. They often do not adjust with the new block of time. Anand goes on to say that he developed a habit of building a pause after Move 40 by going for a walk and getting some water or coffee to re-centre himself before proceeding further. DJ goes on to say, 'We may not be playing chess at the highest level but if we think hard enough, I feel we all can find the equivalent of Move 40 in our lives and build a proactive pause.'

What a wonderful metaphor for the messy midlife!

DJ's unparalleled primary research along with the tribulations of the reader and the life example of the author are three reasons to read this book.

For thousands of years, philosophers have written and thought about how to be happy. For the last 100 years since Chesterton's diatribe, many more have written books on success. DJ's book on potential is somewhat different; it guides us to a life of fulfilment by working towards success within the ambit of our abilities. When success is not relative, it is an enabler and not a detractor to happiness.

To quote DJ himself early on his book: 'In the same segment of the conversation, Vijay Amritraj also referred to Late Thurgood Marshall, American Supreme Court's first African–American justice. When Thurgood Marshall was asked how he would like to be remembered when he is no more, he is known to have said the following: "I would like to be remembered as 'he did what he could with what he had'." I haven't come across a pithier definition of what striving to play to full potential could mean.'

Neither have I.

Sudhir Sitapati                                    Mumbai,
                                                   7 July 2024

# Introduction

If you go to Amazon.com and search for 'potential', I am pretty sure you will see more than a thousand book suggestions. This begs the question, why should you care about this book and what makes it different?

If we look around, many awards celebrate precocity and early achievement. For instance, there are 40 under 40 and 30 under 30 awards that showcase how individuals have achieved so much within a very short period. I have nothing against celebrating individuals who are hitting the ball out of the park when it comes to professional outcomes. We need these people to shake up the world and inspire other people. Given the nature of some of these individuals, they are often 'all in' in their pursuits and often compromise on other aspects like health, relationships etc. Mahatma Gandhi was known as the Father of the Nation but had a troubled relationship with his sons. Had he prioritized work–life harmony, I am not sure if India would have gained independence. There is often a larger cause and purpose that consumes such driven individuals. Let us call this group Type 1. Elon Musk is a contemporary example of this kind of individual. Somebody who has a transformative vision for the future and is willing to burn the candle at both ends (and more) in pursuit of that vision. These people are likely to define potential as something that is expressed in service of a larger-than-life cause that they deeply care about. We do need these individuals who are at the cutting edge of transforming the world we live in. They make the world worth living in.

However, in my journey, I have noticed that Type 1s might possibly be a minority in every society. There is possibly a much larger section of people who are looking to lead a life of balance and meaning. People who define potential in a multi-dimensional sense that includes impact, career, family, health, happiness and much more. Do not get me wrong. They are keen to do well professionally and have a desire to contribute towards wider social impact. However, they do not wish to go 'all in'. They do not make professional success their only mission, while sacrificing everything else. They are looking to unlock their full potential as human beings, especially through the pulls and pressures of midlife. Let us call these individuals Type 2. I firmly place myself in this category.

I would not like to place any value judgement on which is better. The world definitely needs both types, but I feel if we take an honest look in the mirror, more often than not, we would be able to place ourselves in one of the two buckets or at least relate to one more than the other. The primary audience for this book is people who identify themselves as Type 2. However, I would like to believe that even some of the Type 1s might benefit from some of the concepts discussed in the book if they take a 'long' view of life.

* * *

The term 'unicorn', a symbol of rarity, is often commonly used to describe an organization that is valued above USD 1 billion. However, I like to think of unicorns differently. I believe that each one of us is a unicorn in our own bespoke way given our traits, beliefs, context, journey, experiences, vision etc., and we are presented with opportunities to embrace this uniqueness and lead a full life. This book shares some perspectives that could get you started on that journey.

## What Do I Mean by Potential?

The term 'potential' conjures up many questions in people's minds. What is my potential? How do I know if I am playing to my potential—is it me or someone else? Who is to determine if I am playing to my potential? Is it me or someone else? What are the markers of me playing to my full potential?

I would like to go back to something I learnt in my very first *Play to Potential* podcast conversation with the tennis legend Vijay Amritraj in December 2016. As I was wrapping up our conversation, I asked him what 'play to potential' meant to him. He shared a couple of perspectives that have stayed with me.

He first referred to one of his visits to Buzz Aldrin's home in California. Buzz Aldrin was the second man to step on the moon after Neil Armstrong. Vijay recounts being struck by one of the plaques on his wall which said, 'Who said sky is the limit when I left my footprints on the moon.' I find this to be a powerful reminder of the fact that human potential is infinite and often limited by our imagination.

In the same segment of the conversation, Vijay also referred to the Late Thurgood Marshall, the American Supreme Court's first African-American justice. When Thurgood Marshall was asked how he would like to be remembered when he was no more, he is known to have said the following: I would like to be remembered as the manifestation of the following phrase: 'He did what he could with what he had.' I haven't come across a pithier definition of what striving to play to full potential could mean.

This book is about helping you do the best you can across the various domains of your life with what you have. I truly believe that if you can accomplish this, you would have played to your potential.

## Where the Perspectives Come From

The thoughts I share in this book come from four broad sources.

**Insights from the *Play to Potential* podcast**

I have been curating the *Play to Potential* podcast[1] since December 2016 and have had the opportunity to speak to 100+ people including business leaders, management thinkers,[2] Olympic athletes, artists and those from other fields. My conversations with these accomplished individuals are often about how they have thought about the two questions, 'where to go' and 'how to grow' at various points in their journey. I feel unlocking potential is as much about picking the mountain to climb as it is about mastering climbing. Through these conversations, I could glean and curate insights around leadership, transitions and careers. This mix of research-backed insights coupled with anecdotal insights from some of the journeys of inspiring leaders has helped me form a nuanced view on this topic.

**Window-seat observations as a search consultant**

I spent close to six years at Egon Zehnder (between 2010 and 2016), a global executive search firm helping companies recruit chief executive officers (CEOs), chief functional officers (CXOs) and board members. Over those six years, I had the unique opportunity to have immersive conversations with more than a thousand leaders. While the primary objective of the conversations was around ascertaining the individual's appetite/suitability for a role, the discussions would often meander into what kept the individual awake at night when it came to their career and life. This experience gave me a rich insight into what makes senior leaders tick, the challenges they face, and how they think about unlocking their full potential.

## Lessons from my journeys with clients

While working with clients as a coach and as a trusted sounding board, conversations often straddle multiple themes across their personal and professional lives, in which they work with me as a sparring partner. Some of the themes include:

- The leadership required in the context of a business role;
- how they think about choices in the context of business and life priorities; and
- Their approach to self-development and personal transformation.

This has given me a unique vantage point into how people think about unlocking full potential.

## My journey

I am just one of the eight billion people on this planet and there is something for us to learn from each one of them. I am mindful of not overmining my journey and deriving too many lessons from it. To the extent possible, I have tried to use lessons from my journey in the context of an insight that might have come from one of these other sources.

Hopefully, you will find this potpourri of insights across the four sources thought-provoking as you go about your journey in discovering and playing to your unique potential.

## Who Might/Might Not Find the Book Valuable

You might find this book valuable if you want to be deliberate in the way you walk through life and not let things happen to you. There are no fancy hacks or thirteen things to do kind of listicles that provide a magic answer. You might appreciate that a lot of the topics discussed in this book are nebulous and bespoke to each individual context. However, this book shares examples of people who have worked with the concepts that we discuss so that you get a sense of how the ideas can be applied.

The book specifically shines light on the long and messy midlife because that is when the pulls and pressures of the various dimensions of life are the highest. That is when we are swimming in the high seas of life without a clear lighthouse in sight. However, some of the ideas in the book could be applied by people at various stages of their life, whether you are a student, early in your career or a retired person.

The book has a default bias of helping provide perspectives that help people play the long game. If you are looking for quick hacks for the short-term, the book is unlikely to be helpful. Most of the themes discussed require consistent effort for some time before you start seeing meaningful changes.

You need to know that I am a fellow traveller like you are and this is a learning journey for me as well. You should not see this book as a testimony of someone who has cracked the puzzle of unlocking potential. It is more a set of reflections from somebody who is a keen student of leadership, transitions and potential. As you would appreciate, I have my own set of biases given my journey and my vantage point. I urge you to apply your own judgement as you consume some of the ideas in this book.

## How to Work with the Book

The book is divided into three sections.

**SECTION A** is about unpacking the various elements of midlife where we really start grappling with the multi-dimensional elements of life. We are often pushed to manage our careers and key relationships in the family, take care of our health and find ways to keep ourselves energized and engaged as we go through this journey.

- *Chapter 1* deconstructs on what makes midlife so messy and why 'solutioning' is hard.
- *Chapter 2* lays out the key challenges with ikigai as a tactical tool while it serves its purpose as a useful North Star.

**SECTION B** is about building awareness of who we are and what matters to us. We all have to recognize our uniqueness. We all must find answers that are specific to us and unless we really embark on the journey of heightened awareness, it would be difficult for us to find meaningful answers.

- *Chapter 3* discusses the criticality of self-awareness given the leadership and transition contexts today and lays out a few tactical steps people can take to be more reflective and mindful and build internal self-awareness.
- *Chapter 4* gets into the nuances of how you can harness the power of feedback and how corporate 360s are such a small element of what you can glean outside-in. We specifically discuss the where, who, what and when of external self-awareness.
- *Chapter 5* outlines some of the approaches we could take to tune into our values and principles. This includes tuning into our regrets, decoding our role models and tuning into the voices of the people who are looking at death in the eye.

Section B is like essential pre-work before we get into the nuts and bolts of living a full life and playing to our full potential.

**SECTION C** of the book gets into the crux of the approach that I suggest for your consideration to be on your way to playing to your full potential.

- ***Chapter 6*** unpacks the notion of FLAVOUR, the various elements of a full life; clearly there is no one right answer here; the key is to solve for coherence across the various dimensions of FLAVOUR and keep rediscovering it as one's life context evolves.
- ***Chapter 7*** gives a peek into six diverse journeys of women and men who are striving to play to their full potential. Some of them are not the type who might be featured on magazine covers. It includes men and women who are playing the best game they can, given the cards they have been dealt.
- ***Chapter 8*** strives to decode some of the meta-skills and mindsets we might need to strive to lead a FLAVOUR-ful life which puts us on a path to unlocking our full potential.
- ***Chapter 9*** discusses some of the approaches we can take to rediscover our FLAVOUR as we go through various transitions in our lives. As we experience different seasons, we need to work to intentionally discover the FLAVOUR of our season.

There is a certain linearity to the book. I would urge you to try and read it chronologically. It will help you get more out of the book than if you directly jumped to a certain chapter.

You will also find audio clips peppered throughout the narrative. Whenever you see (🎤), it indicates that there is a curated audio clip that you can listen to if you want to hear it in the words of the experts themselves. My team and I have painstakingly culled out those segments for your listening from the *Play to Potential* podcast that we have been curating since 2016. We hope that this multimedia approach is of value in your assimilating the insight. I will strive to describe the crux of the insight in the text of the book. But there might be some nuances that you might find of value when you listen to the related audio clip that accompanies the insight. Chapter 7 has six case studies of women and men who are leading FLAVOUR-ful lives. We also have video interviews with these individuals for you to get a sense of how they got here; links of which are embedded in the chapter.

Given the nature of the topics the book covers, driving change in these areas can be a slow process. I urge you to be patient with yourself as you work through the themes. It might even be a good idea to pause at the end of every chapter, marinate in it, reflect on it, and possibly even take some action in that dimension before you move forward. You might also find that having another person (spouse, friend or a team member) read the book might help in discussing some of the themes and determine the implications of that in your life.

# SECTION A

 **THE LONG AND MESSY MIDLIFE**

 GETTING IN TOUCH WITH OURSELVES

 AN APPROACH TO A FULL LIFE

# 1

# The Midlife Conundrum

*I walk a lonely road*
*The only one that I have ever known*
*Don't know where it goes*
*But it's home to me, and I walk alone*
—'Boulevard of Broken Dreams', Green Day

Midlife has traditionally been described as the passage of play between the forties and fifties but given that we live longer, and that our lives are getting more complex and non-linear, some of the phenomena that are typically attributed to midlife could possibly be felt by people in their thirties and sixties. It is that phase where we are at least about five to ten years into our working life and have five to ten years of working life ahead of us. One could call it the high seas of our working life where no lighthouse is to be seen for comfort.

It is also that phase of life when people's mental and physical bandwidths are often choked because of a triple whammy. This is often the time when:

a)  work life is the most intense;
b)  kids are at the phase where they demand a lot of time; and
c)  parents start ageing and require greater attention to their health issues.

As a student of leadership, journeys and transitions, I have observed that all of us encounter these turbulent passages of play in our lives where multiple things come together across our professional and personal fronts and cause a knot that seems hard to unpick. How we engage with this messiness can determine our life outcomes.

In these situations, I have seen the script play out in three broad ways. In the worst-case scenario, people get into a vicious loop and implode. In the moderate case, they end up chugging along, often over-indexing on one or two domains of life till there is an event that hits them and forces them to reprioritize. In some rare cases, people seem to be proactive about engaging the multiple dimensions and end up leading a fulfilling life of happiness and meaning.

To go back to the visual of the high seas, these three scenarios are equivalent to sinking, drifting or swimming. This book strives to share some of the lessons that might be useful in swimming with intent in the high seas of life.

However, we must understand the dynamics of midlife and why it might come about before we move to discussing the potential ways in which we can turn it from a crisis to an opportunity.

In this chapter, we look at the various reasons behind midlife angst, and why we struggle to solve it meaningfully. In the next chapter, we will look at some approaches to deal with it. Sometimes, understanding the shape of the problem is critical before we move to solutioning.

## Unpacking Midlife

I have noticed that midlife shows up differently in various people's lives. Some of the questions I come across include:

- I have all the money I need or want for the rest of my life. How do I spend the time that I have left? How do I make sense of the world of possibilities out there?
- I was pursuing a career but post-maternity, I focused on my family and kids. Now that I am an empty nester, how do I spend my time meaningfully?
- I love my work, but I can't sustain the lifestyle, my health is taking a beating and/or I don't get any time with family.
- My daily job is so hectic that I don't have the time to think about 'what else'. I want to take a break but how will the job market look at me if I take a six-month

sabbatical to figure things out? I feel I will lose relevance quickly.

- I feel like I am stuck in the wrong career. Where do I go from here?
- I am making decent money but seem to be missing my purpose. What is my why?
- I just turned fifty—I would like to make the next innings of my career really count and finish with a flourish.

When we encounter these questions, I notice that we often do not know where to start.

Let us first look at why we experience this midlife phenomenon, and about its timing—that we don't experience too early or too late in our lives.

### Availability of big data

By the time we approach midlife, we might have collected several experiences, some real data to reflect upon. We all grew up reflecting on the question 'what do you want to become when you grow up?' I have come to realize that it is a challenging question to navigate early on in life (for that matter at any point in our lives) because we don't have a realistic understanding of what we would enjoy and what we would be skilled at. However, by the time we approach midlife, we often have enough data to work with for sense-making. Chances are we have possibly lived in a few places, tried a few jobs and dealt with a few work cultures. In addition, we see journeys around us unfolding that provide further data for us to reflect on.

## The 'Maslow Shift'

Very often, people have moved levels in terms of where they are on Maslow's Hierarchy of Needs.[1] Our needs slowly shift as we move up the pyramid. To understand how this plays out in people's lives, let us work with three variables— money (surrogate for earnings/wealth), needs (what we can live with) and wants (the master list of whatever we would like to have if finances were not a constraint). This is a gross simplification of the problem but just for illustration, let us work with these three. There are three feasible permutations to these three variables (assuming wants > needs).

A) Wants > needs > money
B) Wants > money > needs
C) Money > wants > needs

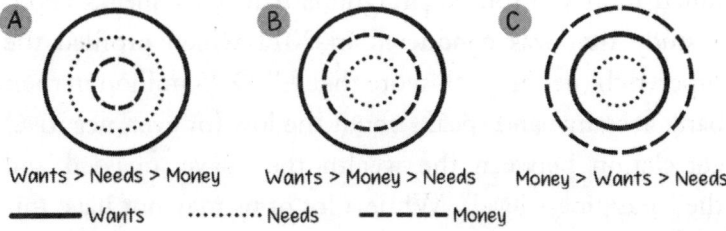

I come from the Indian middle class. I saw several people around me who grew up in scenario A or scenario B but as they experienced commercial success in their twenties, thirties and forties, they moved to scenario C. If you started in scenario C, then you might have experienced less of a Maslow Shift as you hit midlife. But the key point to note is that the relationship between money and our wants and needs has an implication on how we think about spending our time and how we prioritize various objectives.

People often have wealth managers. But at high levels of wealth, the real question is often, 'Given I have all the money to take care of my wants, how do I spend my time (i.e. What do I do with my life?)?' Once people move to scenario C, I have noticed that the correlation between happiness and fulfilment (although they mean different things, I have clubbed them here to make a broader point) and wealth accumulation is often much weaker than their correlation with the choices you make around how you spend time. You can see the diminishing marginal utility of money playing out as you move from scenario A to B to C. In a lot of instances, there is often a negative utility of too much money. Prof. Raj Raghunathan[2] (🎤[3]) speaks about a study that was conducted in 2011 which profiled the super-rich (people with more than USD 25 million in their bank account) and speaks about the low (or even negative) correlation between the wealth they have amassed and their happiness levels. While a lot of us may not have this kind of money, midlife is the time when we often are re-examining our relationship with money and that can lead to its own set of upheavals and challenges depending on where we are, how the people in our family think, and what the constraints and opportunities are. And this churn can cause a lot of angst.

## The astronaut syndrome

Sometimes, success can be dramatic and can catapult people into a different orbit. Tony Robbins, an American author, coach and speaker, uses the term 'Astronaut Syndrome' to describe the phenomenon that some people experience when they achieve dramatic, early success (like with an initial public offering [IPO], a deal, an exit or some such financial transaction). Let us say that you always dreamed of becoming an astronaut since your childhood. What if you get to go to the moon and back when you are in your early thirties. Where do you go from there? Avnish Bajaj (🎤), now a venture investor at Matrix Partners, makes the point about how everything changed for him at thirty-three when he sold the business he had built, Baazee, to eBay for USD 55 million. He says that the event suddenly changed everything for him. He had set a target of USD 2 million for himself, and he suddenly found himself with a multiple of this number. He had all the money he wanted (and some more). Now he had to figure out what to do with the rest of his life.

## Micro-shifts in our preferences over time

If I go back to my journey, I started as a management consultant in London. As a twenty-something-year-old, visiting a new city, experiencing a new culture and being in a different geography between Monday and Friday was exciting and fun. But the same lifestyle has a very different implication today. The lure of flight travel is not as exciting as it used to be. Travel today also means separation from family and time away from the kids. Something similar could be said about the intensity of the hours at work. Working till 11 p.m. or midnight, day after day, is exciting and good for learning and career growth in the early years (some might argue that even this is not worth it but that is a separate discussion) but as time wears on, it starts taking a toll on the health of the individual and their relationships.

Travel and intensity are just two elements that I have mentioned but several assumptions that we make in our twenties about costs and benefits don't hold when we move into our thirties, forties and beyond. The equations begin to change across multiple dimensions. Very often, this is not a discrete shift but a slow 'frog in boiling water' situation where the temperature keeps rising one degree at a time. We don't notice the implication in the short run but slowly the costs begin to add up in terms of our health/relationships. While this is happening, we are also often slowly evolving in parallel.

## Transition towards self-authorship

Dr Robert (Bob) Kegan, a developmental psychologist and professor at Harvard University, has studied adult development extensively. His model of adult development includes several transitions and stages. Here is a short synthesis of how we evolve.

The first stage is the 'impulsive' mind. This is in early childhood where the individual is driven by their impulses and cannot quite differentiate their inner feelings from external realities. The second stage is the 'imperial' mind which is the phase of adolescence during which there is a tendency to be self-centric. The individual might recognize others' feelings but choose to prioritize their own needs. The third stage is the 'socialized' mind which often begins in late adolescence. In this stage, people seek external validation and are heavily influenced by the expectations and norms of others. The fourth stage is the 'self-authoring' mind. Here, individuals craft their own belief systems, independent of external influences. They become self-directed, managing conflicts between values and setting priorities based on personal beliefs. The fifth and final stage is 'self-transforming' mind. This is a stage where individuals see the multiple facets of issues, recognizing their own perspective as one of many. They embrace interconnectedness, are comfortable with contradictions, and constantly re-evaluate deeply held beliefs. The real interesting insight for me is that he goes on to say that about 58 per cent of adults are still in stage 3, being governed by the Joneses while 35 per cent are in stage 4. Less than 1 per cent make it to stage 5.[4] A lot of the angst in the midlife is often about people trying to transition from stage 3 to stage 4 as we try to move from an outside-in frame of life to an inside-out frame. And that is a non-trivial transition. If handling our own transition was not enough, more lives start getting enmeshed with ours as time elapses.

**Turning a bicycle or steering a ship**

When we are in our twenties and set out into our careers, we often aren't accountable for too many other variables apart from our own lives. We are accountable for our decisions, and we deal with the consequences. It is also easy to change trajectory and move locations for a new opportunity if we want to.

As we grow older, other variables start appearing in our life—people in our organization that have bet their careers on us, investors who have backed us, spouse who might also be pursuing a career, children who require time and attention and ageing parents, just to name a few. A couple of things happen here. First, the decision-making gets complex because there are multiple expectations to be considered. Even if one cuts through the clutter and gets to a decision that makes sense 'all things considered', we are still left with the task of being thoughtful about the 'how' in terms of getting the stakeholders aligned and moving forward. There is a chance that we might still make the right decision but the people around us might be unhappy because we haven't navigated the 'how to get there' tactfully. The other piece I have observed is that this might also be a phase where your emotional bank balance may run low with some of the family members because we have been running full throttle on the work front. So, our ability to influence them with our thoughts and suggestions (even if it is the right outcome for them) is limited possibly because you haven't had the time and the mindspace to build credit in the account over the years.

While most of us are taught to ride a bicycle, we aren't necessarily taught how to manoeuvre a ship. And that can feel unnerving as we navigate in the choppy high seas of midlife with a boat full of passengers who we are often accountable for. Some of the passengers might also be indulging in back-seat driving which makes the navigation even more challenging.

## Why Do We Often Get Stuck with Midlife Challenges

While we have considered a lot of factors which could lead to midlife angst, it is as important to recognize why we struggle to solve them meaningfully. The human mind is built to deal with a lot of complex problems, but somehow, we still seem to struggle when it comes to resolving some of the issues that come up around midlife.

### Inertia leading to perpetuating status quo

At this point in time, several people are often motoring along at a good clip and there is good commercial momentum. Several financial needs are taken care of, and material comfort is well provided for. But we know in our heart that the path we are on, may not make sense in the medium to long run. A few common reasons include:

a) There is toxicity and politics at the top which make it less fun; you start wondering if it is all worth it.

b) We are not enjoying it as much as we did earlier
   (you have hit the diminishing curve of learning
   and fun).
c) The lifestyle of the profession is not sustainable beyond
   a point. Some of the balance sheet metrics such as
   health and relationships are taking a hit.

But given the comfort of good cash flows today, you
often don't want to act on the erosion of health and
relationships that are likely to negatively impact you in the
future. This is because you don't know what the next best
option is in these circumstances. Leaders often want to
take a sabbatical to figure out choices and solve this puzzle
but the risk of not finding a landing pad at the end of
a sabbatical comes in the way and they end up motoring
along despite the dissonance.

The other factor that leads to prolonging the status
quo is sensitivity and confidentiality. Leaders who attain
a certain level of success also have a market reputation to
protect. If they are seen accessing the job market, word
can get around very quickly and it can come in the way
of their credibility in their current organization. Given
this, several leaders end up having a very low opening
of the aperture when it comes to accessing the world of
opportunity. The high opportunity cost, risk aversion
given what is at stake and confidentiality act as strong
frictional forces which come in the way of accessing
new horizons.

**Inability/unwillingness to process the inner world**

I realize that we are a function of the context in which we grow up. If we were zebras in the Serengeti Plains, we may not have the luxury of meditating if we want to survive. I feel it is a similar phenomenon at play in a country like India which faces resource scarcity. Being competitive and doing better than others was a prerequisite for a lot of us to access the world of opportunity. If you are in a famine-stricken country and you see a helicopter with food packets, you don't question what is in the food packet. You just grab it. A lot of us from the middle class were told that there were a few institutes of eminence worth enrolling into and those were the passport to a better life. And we scrambled towards those food packets without really questioning it too much because it felt like the right thing to do.

A lot of the education we were exposed to (some of it is changing in select pockets) was about processing the external world. But nobody really taught a lot of us how to listen to our inner voice. We discuss this in the chapters on self-awareness. I wonder how much of it is a skill versus a will issue. I feel it is a combination of both. Even if we turn our gaze inwards, there are a few challenges here.

a) The inside world is often a fuzzy combination of thoughts that are circulating in our system. It is hard to put structure and language around it. The lack of objective metrics in the inner world compared to the outer world makes it harder.

b) We see ourselves with tinted glasses. It is often hard to be objective about oneself.

c) Even if we can accurately process the inner world, map it to our external context and know what needs to be done, there is a challenge in translating some of those thoughts into action (knowing–doing gap).

Constructive, nuanced and thoughtful workplace feedback is often hard to come by and even if it does, it is often anchored around what you do well, and what you could do differently in that specific work context. The feedback is themed around the 'how to grow'. But in midlife, you are also seeking to gain clarity about what energizes you, which is one of the key determinants of resolving the 'where to go' of your journey.

### 'Where to go' is a strategy project that requires resources

Imagine you are the CEO of a company, and you are looking for external help in putting together the company strategy. Would you craft the strategy by having coffee conversations with a few people who know your company well and can give you an idea or two? Putting a strategy together would require building a nuanced understanding of the context of the company, its resources, the vision, the realities of the marketplace and more before crafting a strategy. You might even hire a strategy consultant to do that.

Just like strategy consultants help companies with the 'where to play', leaders often need somebody they trust to understand their complete context so that they act as a sounding board on the 'where to go'. But very often they tend to navigate this question on their own with suboptimal advice (based on limited data). Friends and family have a lot of data about you but often don't have the ability or perspective to guide you. The mentors (seasoned leaders who end up becoming your well-wishers) often have the wisdom but don't have access to the detailed data or the context required to help with decision-making. Last but not least, each of these cohorts of people has seen a certain pathway play out in their case and that lack of imagination can rub off on the leader going through his/her midlife.

People in your current company are busy trying to fit you into the organization or their notion of a career and aren't necessarily solving for your context. Their advice around what makes sense for you is often biased because if you are a good performer, they want to retain you at all costs.

The challenge is that leaders have access to the best of pedigreed and reputed professional advisory firms when they are solving for their company. They often are left to deal with an 'unorganized sector' when it comes to crafting their own life strategy. Advisory services firms often exist to serve other organizations. You get good advice for your role but not for yourself. We all know it is lonely at the top. I have noticed that it gets lonelier when individuals are trying to navigate their career through various twists and turns.

Net-net, you are left to make sense of all these points of view across the various dimensions and that can be quite

overwhelming especially when you have limited mental
bandwidth to be thoughtful about it.

## Limited mindspace to problem-solve the
## real issues

Edward Hallowell wrote an interesting *Harvard Business
Review* article (published in 2005) titled 'Overloaded
Circuits: Why smart people underperform'. He says that
the cerebral cortex in the brain is responsible for complex
executive tasks (thinking about the long-term, making
tough decisions, being nuanced in our communication
with people, thoughtfulness in our choices etc.). He says
that once we load the brain beyond a point, it quickly
starts sending the signals to the inner core. That part
of the brain behaves a little more like an animal in the
wild. The typical response to a problem is fight, fright
or flight.

Given the number of moving parts across careers,
parents' and our children's lives, our mind is often
overloaded leading to us operating in 'animal mode'. To
further amplify the problem, given the proliferation of
electronic devices and social media, any buffer time which
would have been a good opportunity for reflection is often
spent by consuming some form of media. While electronic
devices and internet connectivity have opened our doors to
the world outside, without us realizing it, they have made
it much harder for us to access our inner world.

## We keep looking for a trapeze

If we think about how the initial few transitions in our life play out, they are like moving from one trapeze to another. Very often we have our hand on the next trapeze before we let go of the current one. We often have our college admission before we finish Class 12. We often have our jobs lined up before we graduate with an MBA degree. The key point to be made is that the options line up concurrently. I have observed that in later years, as one gets senior and the possibility set widens, the options do not necessarily line up cleanly like a buffet in a restaurant. When I was working as a search consultant at Egon Zehnder, I would speak to successful leaders about an opportunity, and I would often see them struggle with the choice because they were being asked to choose between their current organization (CurrentCo) and the new opportunity (NewCo). What makes it harder is that in these conversations, CurrentCo and NewCo are trying to discern, 'Are you a good value add to the company and the role? But you are trying to determine, 'Is this role right for me given my unique context?' And that is a very different question. Very often, what you are looking for may not exist as a ready role in another company. It might have to be 'cooked' for a period of time for that possibility to become real. Very often we do not have the mindspace or the bandwidth to cultivate something like this to bear fruit a few years down the line. We hesitate to take a sabbatical/break as we fear being perceived as low on ambition. This is the equivalent of a discomforting feeling of weightlessness when you leave one trapeze, and you don't have anything to hold on to. Prolonging the status quo seems comforting and practical given all this.

## Lack of a 'catch-all' metric to measure progress

A lot of us start out by using compensation as a yardstick of progress and success in the early years. That gives us a false sense of comfort early on. But as time elapses and we move up Maslow's Hierarchy of Needs, money starts having diminishing utility and other elements come into play (health, relationships, vitality, purpose, impact etc.) which begin to matter. Not having a clear answer to 'how am I doing' can be unnerving without a clear all-encompassing metric that captures our complete situation. By default, we often end up benchmarking ourselves to our peer group and keep measuring our performance against that cohort. Once again, the bespoke metric (if at all) possibly lies within but we keep looking for it externally.

Even if I look at the recent spurt in running in the corporate world in India (as compared to some of the other forms of exercise), I wonder if it is because people get to have one visible metric to measure and signal progress and compete—the time you take to complete the run. Once you have a target, you start working on it and chip away at it because you have done that all your life. But pursuing things like yoga, meditation or going to the gym don't necessarily give you metrics to track and that can feel unsettling to the

Type As—people who are wired to chase metrics. Solving one metric gives us a false sense of comfort and control.

For all the reasons we have discussed in this chapter around the complex nature of midlife coupled with the challenges in resolving it, we end up wallowing in midlife angst. Very often, in these situations, ikigai is suggested to people as a panacea. In the next chapter, we will see that while ikigai is a useful 30,000-foot guide, we might need something more granular to navigate the messiness of midlife.

## Contextual Audio Snippets from the Podcast

- **Audio clip 1.1**: Prof. Raj Raghunathan on the secret fears of the super rich
- **Audio clip 1.2**: Avnish Bajaj speaks about how he was at a crossroads when he sold Baazee to Ebay for USD 55 million

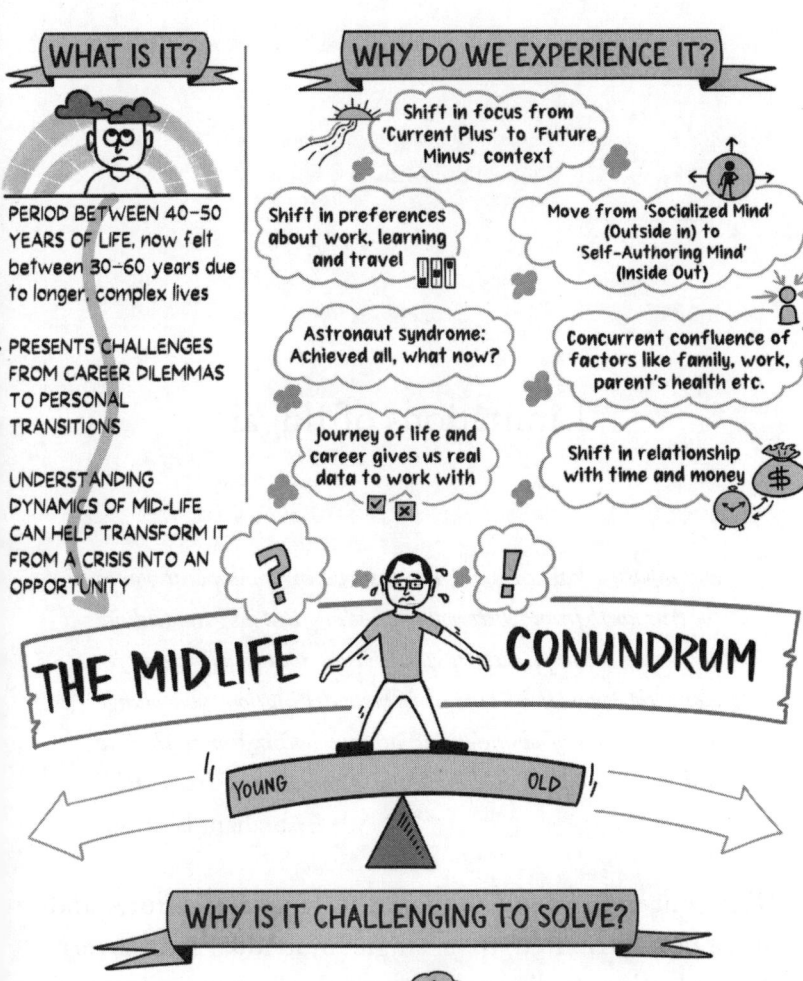

# 2

# Limitations of Ikigai

*A compass, I learned while I was surveying, will point you to the true north from where you're standing. But it's got no advice about the swamps, deserts and chasms that you'll encounter along the way. If in pursuit of your destination, you plunge ahead heedless of obstacles and achieve nothing more than to sink in a swamp . . . what's the use of knowing the true north?*

—Abraham Lincoln[1]

The concept of ikigai is rooted in Japanese culture, and it is not attributed to a single individual's discovery. Instead, it's a traditional concept that's been an integral part of Japanese societal values for centuries. It is often seen as the thing that explains longevity and vitality as people live long lives in certain parts of Japan, especially around Okinawa. Many other cultures have a similar concept—Ancient Greece had a concept called *eudaimonia* which speaks about the notion of human flourishing and denotes a life of balance, virtue and wisdom, aiming to achieve the highest human good. In Costa Rica, *pura vida*[2], literally translated to 'pure life', describes the laidback, optimistic and contented way of life. In Scandinavia, *hygge*, (pronounced hoo-guh) refers to a mood of coziness, comfort and well-being. It emphasizes simple pleasures and is often associated with family, friends and a sense of contentment. While many approaches exist around the world, ikigai seems to have captured the imagination[3] of several people around the world, especially when it comes to the notion of playing to one's full potential.

The crux of the ikigai way of life is to find the holy grail—the intersection of four different elements (as illustrated in the image below).

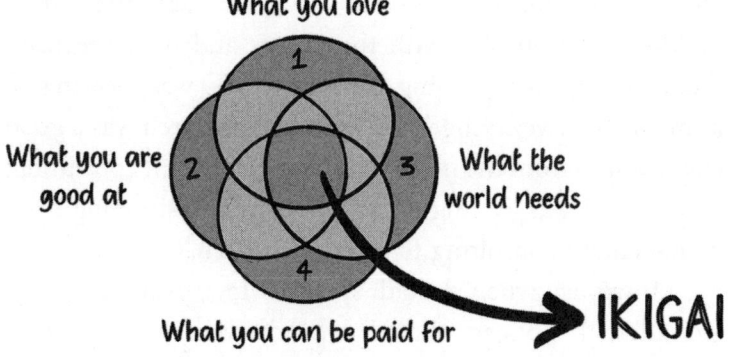

## My Journey with Ikigai

In 2016, when I moved out from my corporate journey at Egon Zehnder to set up my independent advisory practice around leadership development and transitions, I used ikigai to clarify my thinking and even recorded a short video clip[4] as my public commitment to the external world so that the people around me could hold me accountable to this. As I thought of the four circles of Ikigai, this was how I related to it back then.

*What you love:* I took the first step towards what I love in 2010, when I moved from McKinsey to Egon Zehnder. McKinsey consultants were often evaluated on 3 dimensions (intellectual quotient [IQ] as demonstrated in problem-solving horsepower in different situations, capability quotient [CQ] as demonstrated in elements such as project planning, quality of communication, modelling capability etc. and relationship quotient [RQ] as demonstrated in building relationships with the clients and with the team members). I was beginning to hear that RQ was showing up as my distinctive strength. I felt executive search was a good exit (for me) from the motorway of management consulting. It felt like I was leaning into my RQ by transitioning from management consulting to executive search.

However, when I had spent a few years at Egon Zehnder, I noticed that I was deriving energy from candidate-counselling conversations where I would advise them on their career pathways. To me, these conversations were more fulfilling than conducting interviews or counselling clients or negotiating the offer with the client or the candidate. However, I discovered that counselling candidates was just a footnote in a search consultant's life. It was not the primary objective. Eventually, I set out from Egon Zehnder to set up my leader-centric advisory practice in 2016. Today, I sense a greater resonance between what I do for a living and what energizes me. To that extent, work feels like play and is energizing rather than draining.

*What the world needs*: We have all heard the cliché, 'It is lonely at the top!' While it was true for leaders in the context of their role in their companies, I observed that it was lonelier when it came to them navigating their journeys. As CEOs and MDs, the leaders could often access advisers who could help them with various topics: marketing, corporate finance, strategy, supply chain or some business-related topics. However, when it came to their solving the 'what next' on their own, they found themselves in a very lonely spot. Given the confidentiality, they often could not discuss this with anyone in the outside world. The family was often not in a position to provide counsel in such a situation. Just like companies are solving 'where to play' and 'how to win' in the context of their strategy, I felt leaders would need help with 'where to go' and 'how to grow'. While many coaches had emerged to address the 'how to grow', helping leaders with their transition felt like a Blue Ocean,[5] a space where there was limited competition. These transitions also felt like the vital few moments where I could be of value. Problems were complex, leaders were lonely, and stakes were high. I felt there was a need for a trusted sounding board in these situations.

***What you are good at***: I had worked in advisory services (at KPMG Consulting, McKinsey and Egon Zehnder) and felt that I had built an appreciation of various business issues in a company. The breadth of exposure gave me an insight into business models and strategic issues across companies. My stint at Egon Zehnder required me to assess an individual's leadership capability in the context of a role including the fit between a company and an individual. Conversations with candidates also gave me a window into the journeys of leaders and what they were solving for. Finally, I noticed that every conversation was a transition conversation—career transition with the candidates and leadership transition with the client. This understanding of business, the leadership in the context of the business and an appreciation of candidate journeys gave me the courage to start my candidate-centric transition advisory when I decided to move from Egon Zehnder.

***What can you be paid for:*** This was the piece I was the least sure of when I stepped off the corporate path. While companies pay a high premium for management consultants and sounding boards for dealing with some of their complex, high-stakes issues, I was unsure if leaders would pay for a sounding board when they were at a crossroads in their journey. I felt that if a leader was solving 'how to grow', their growth would benefit the company, hence the company could pick the tab. However, if they were solving 'where to go', it was a personal problem, and the fee was likely to come from the leader's personal pocket. Most advisory firms around the world are often set up around helping organizations (as corporate profit pools are much deeper than personal savings pools). However, I told myself that I was not looking to set up a large advisory firm with many partners. I was trying to be an independent advisor and provide for my family. I felt being a surgeon would bring me greater joy than building a hospital. I was also solving for greater control over the 'flywheel' of life and being an independent advisor, I felt, would give me that control.

However, despite the seeming market opportunity, I felt that it was still a risk I was taking as the field of coaching was clearly not as lucrative as management consulting or executive search—two professions I had been a part of. I am grateful to my wife, Kamini, who came to support me at this crucial juncture. We gave ourselves an eighteen-month stop-loss point to say that if in a year and a half, I didn't have meaningful commercial traction, I could cut losses and return to the corporate pathway. We also decided to lower our expenses and be frugal with our lifestyle just to give ourselves psychological comfort in those times. It helped that we came from backgrounds where fiscal prudence was the norm. My father had been a public sector banker and her father had been an army officer.

I am grateful for the way the journey has played out to date. I feel the work I do is energizing, commercially meaningful and purposeful. It has also given me the ability to pace myself at the intensity that seems right for me given my current phase of life. The ikigai framework helped to make a set of choices that has put me on a path that has got me here.

However, over the last few years, I have had an opportunity to observe this phenomenon through my coaching and sounding board advisory work, insights from the podcast and just by observing the world around me as a student of journeys and transitions. This has led to my becoming a little cautious about applying ikigai to our lives.

## The Limitations of Ikigai

I have come to realize that people's pursuit of ikigai is a lot messier than we often imagine. Ikigai serves as a good true north for us to look at and align our lives in a broad direction in the context of the arc of our life. But very often, we might find ourselves in a swamp or staring at the precipice of a mountain. Having a true north is unlikely to help in the short term. If at all, it might end up causing damage. If someone asked you to look at the sky and use the compass (which points to the true north) to find your way out of a traffic jam, the advice might be conceptually true for the long-term but contextually quite inappropriate at the moment. I find that sometimes we need something that is a bit more granular that accounts for the messiness of our daily lives and helps us resolve these logjams. As I think about playing to our full potential, I have come to realize that there are some challenges with using ikigai as a governing framework. I have seen people having a few disconnects when it comes to applying ikigai in their context.

## Role of context

When I was a student at IIM Ahmedabad, the professors who taught us using the case-based method would say that to solve a situation in life, we would need to have two skills—conceptual clarity and contextual familiarity. I have come to realize that while conceptual frameworks are taught on campus, contextual familiarity takes years to build. Very often the choices we make are in the context of how life unfolds for us and the most important people around us. A framework like ikigai is conceptually sound akin to a true north that can guide us in a certain direction but it doesn't account for the context and messiness of daily lives.

## Daunting and intimidating

Ikigai suggests a 'sweet spot' at the intersection of the four circles. It urges us to try and get there over time. I have found that while it inspires 1 per cent of people who, somehow, can get to what feels like the bull's eye of the Venn diagram, 99 per cent of people I encounter find it disillusioning. It feels like Mount Everest to a lot of people who would be happy if they could complete a trek in Lonavala given their context.

When my daughter turned fourteen in 2023, I got her to see the movie *Poorna: Courage Has No Limit*. The movie is the story of Poorna Malavath, the youngest Indian and youngest girl to climb Mount Everest against all odds. It is a monumental achievement and a well-made movie, but my daughter's response to the movie was quite similar to how a lot of people react to ikigai. If I had to verbalize her thoughts after watching the movie, it would have been something along the lines of 'good for her, but I am thinking how I can solve this problem on fractions'! I notice people having a similar approach to ikigai. It feels a bit daunting and utopian to several, and if they come across somebody who seems to be operating at the intersection their reaction often seems to be 'I am happy for you' rather than 'how can I make it work for me'!

**What about the team?**

The ikigai approach (implicitly) suggests that we solve this jigsaw as individuals. However, I notice that a lot of us end up making choices around our lives (whether it is professional or personal) in the context of our family situation. If you are born into wealth or if your spouse has done well commercially, then 'what you can be paid for' is not relevant. When I look at people who are leading a full life, I notice that they make choices that are in tune with the family—whether it is the financial context, careers of the spouse, phase of life of children or parents. To use a music-related metaphor, the family is often playing the background base note or the underlying chord, and we are trying to make our melody on top of it. The key is to be in harmony and not be jarring to the emerging context. Ikigai doesn't somehow explicitly shine light on that family context which seems to be such a key element of choice. It also doesn't explicitly refer to us investing in our family in our various roles as a spouse, parent, child and sibling.

## Life keeps flowing

Another challenge with ikigai is that it seems to suggest 'the answer', which can give people the illusion that 'I have arrived'. One of my friends uses the term 'I have struck oil' to describe their experience of having found the sweet spot, implicitly indicating that she could continue drilling there for the rest of her life. I have empirically found that life keeps evolving, and in various ways, we need to keep re-architecting our life as we go through the various transitions that we encounter, whether expected or unexpected. Just like in a cricket match, we need to have a certain approach to a 'passage of play', we often need to find an approach that is fit for purpose for a phase of life and that the answer might evolve over time as various transitions unfold (maternity, retirement, empty nesting, divorce, loss of a spouse, parents falling ill, health episode etc.) in our lives and that of the loved ones around us.

## Passion and purpose are often emergent and not the starting point

An element of ikigai that a lot of people trip over is the way they interpret the role of passion (what one loves) and purpose (what the world needs) in finding the sweet spot. I see a lot of people trying to find what they love at their workplace. I feel many people do not have the luxury of doing that and sometimes must do jobs that they may not fully love to drive cash flows given their context. Papa CJ (🎤), a renowned stand-up comedian, speaks about his transition phase post an MBA from Oxford and a brief career in management consulting when he was early in his journey in stand-up comedy and trying to break into the circuit. He speaks about how he took up a job in a recruitment firm to pay the bills and fund his passion for stand-up till he got to a point where he was able to support himself with earnings from comedy.

Similarly, I find people struggling with the questions such as 'what does the world need' or 'what is your purpose'. They feel too lofty for the common man! It is a bit like asking a five-year-old what he/she wants to become when they are fifty. I have noticed that often the purpose is emergent and is not the starting point. Purpose often reveals itself as we go on the journey of life. We discover it as we walk the path.

Depending on our context, very often we might have to keep our passion in the backdrop and focus on commercial outcomes. Maslow's Hierarchy of Needs is real and there is something to be said about taking care of the basics before we start focusing on our passion. I find that a lot of us go through a phase where we end up operating at the intersection of circles 2 and 4 (what you are good at and what you can be paid for) till we get to a point of financial security. It is another matter that people sometimes get sucked into this vortex but never come out of it. But when somebody is going through this period of accumulating wealth or building experience and possibly doing things that they don't necessarily love completely, it can feel jarring to ask them to seek 'what they love doing' at work. I come across a lot of people who seem to be leading a full life, who are pursuing their passion outside of work which they like (may not love it). They have other activities outside of work—music, painting, gardening, theatre, travel or sport that help them rejuvenate and come back energized at work. There is something to be said about the timing of when we switch completely to our passion. You do it too early and you might end up burning yourself and cause irreparable damage to you and your family. That sense of timing is quite nuanced and quite context specific.

**Personal balance sheet**

There is enough research to suggest that given the advances in healthcare, we all are likely to live long lives. Lynda Gratton[6] (🎙) speaks about how we all are likely to live up to a 100 and are likely to be working through our seventies and eighties. A key element of that is health. If we want to build a company that lasts, then we need to start focusing on our balance sheet and our assets and give that as much or more importance than the P&L. In order to play the long game, Lynda Gratton speaks about three types of intangible assets that we need to pay attention to—productive assets, vitality assets and transformative assets. Productive assets are our skills and capabilities that help us drive value today. Vitality assets refer to our physical and mental health and our ability to handle stress and manage intensity in our lives. Transformative assets are the set of assets that will help us stay relevant in the future. This includes skills, mindsets and relationships.

Ikigai, in a way, focuses on 'what' we could be doing. However, if we are striving to play to our full potential over the long game, how we play it and the intensity with which we play it becomes as important. How we pace our innings for a test match must be different from how we plan a T-20 innings!

While ikigai is useful as a true north, it is distant and difficult to relate to for many. It is useful to keep it at the back of our heads as an overall framework for the long term. But for the short-term, we need something more granular and something we can relate to. Something that recognizes the messiness of the lives we lead.

Section C of this book presents an approach that could help us get moving in the direction of playing to our full potential as we go through the various seasons of life.

But before we go there, I think there is some significant inner work that we all need to do. Section B of this book is about us getting in touch with ourselves and embracing our uniqueness. Once we do the inner work and get to know ourselves, we can embark on a journey to (re)discovering a FLAVOUR that is fit for purpose given our bespoke context, something we explore in detail in chapters 6, 7, 8 and 9.

## Contextual Audio Snippets from the Podcast

- **Audio Clip 2.1**: Papa CJ on balancing pragmatism with passion
- **Audio Clip 2.2**: Lynda Gratton on *The 100-Year Life* and need to focus on intangible assets

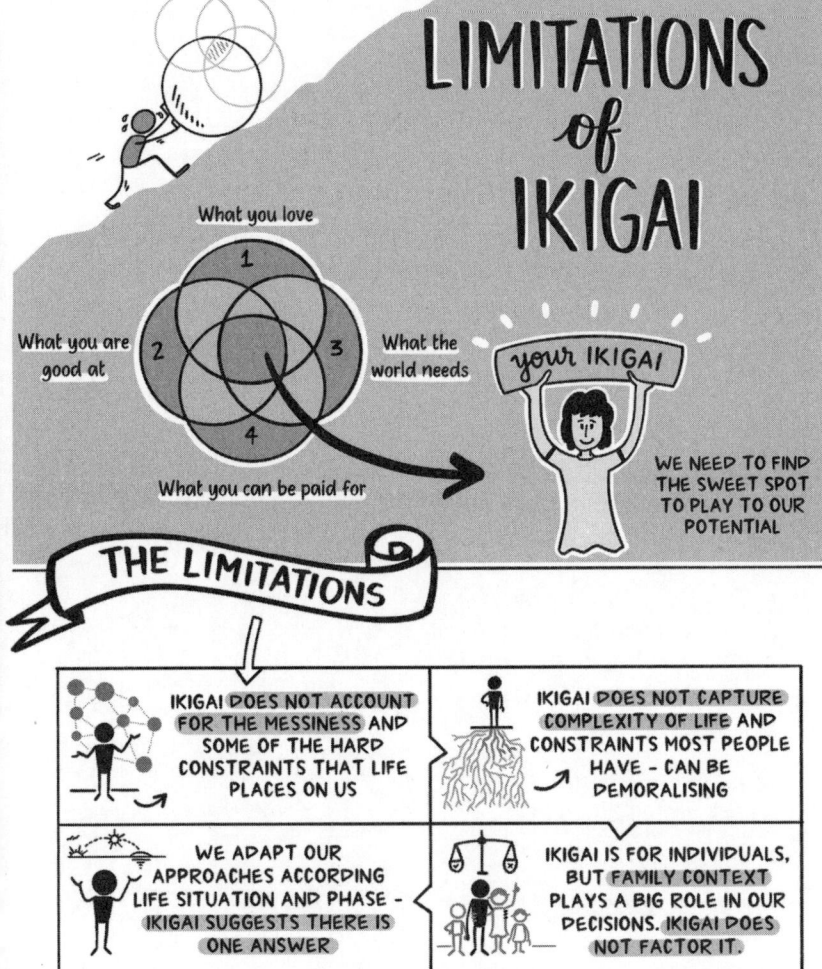

# LIMITATIONS of IKIGAI

What you love

1

What you are good at

2     3     What the world needs

4

What you can be paid for

your IKIGAI

WE NEED TO FIND THE SWEET SPOT TO PLAY TO OUR POTENTIAL

## THE LIMITATIONS

IKIGAI DOES NOT ACCOUNT FOR THE MESSINESS AND SOME OF THE HARD CONSTRAINTS THAT LIFE PLACES ON US

IKIGAI DOES NOT CAPTURE COMPLEXITY OF LIFE AND CONSTRAINTS MOST PEOPLE HAVE – CAN BE DEMORALISING

WE ADAPT OUR APPROACHES ACCORDING LIFE SITUATION AND PHASE – IKIGAI SUGGESTS THERE IS ONE ANSWER

IKIGAI IS FOR INDIVIDUALS, BUT FAMILY CONTEXT PLAYS A BIG ROLE IN OUR DECISIONS. IKIGAI DOES NOT FACTOR IT.

PASSION AND PURPOSE ARE EMERGENT, AND NOT ALWAYS CLEAR AT THE OUTSET

IKIGAI SEEMS TO BE ABOUT WHAT AND LESS ABOUT HOW

# SECTION B

 THE LONG AND MESSY MIDLIFE

 **GETTING IN TOUCH WITH OURSELVES**

 AN APPROACH TO A FULL LIFE

# 3

# What Lies Beneath

*I'm starting with the man in the mirror*
*I'm asking him to change his ways*
*And no message could've been any clearer*
*If they wanna make the world a better place*
*Take a look at yourself and then make a change*
          —Michael Jackson; song: 'Man in the Mirror'

I left the corporate treadmill in 2016 and set up my coaching and advisory practice, my initial hypothesis was that people who were low on self-awareness would reach out seeking help to open some blind spots they had and improve their effectiveness. As time went by, I noticed that the leaders who reached out to me were already significantly self-aware and were doing well in their journeys. These individuals didn't quite need the services of a coach, but they still wanted to strive to become a better version of themselves.

I was puzzled by this phenomenon for a long time. Now, I feel I have a sense of why this might be happening.

## The Paradox of Self-Awareness

While working with leaders, I have noticed that people's ability to self-diagnose their level of self-awareness is often quite skewed. It is quite like a 'drunk person in a party' situation. The drunk person is often not aware that he or she is inebriated. The people around the person know it but are often polite about it. And therein lies the paradox.

I notice that the truly self-aware have a learner's mindset when it comes to understanding themselves and show a sense of humility and healthy discontent with how much they know about themselves. The not-so-self-aware often have a smug misplaced confidence and an 'I have it all figured out' mindset when it comes to curiosity about themselves.

I came across the phenomenon of the Dunning-Kruger Effect sometime back in the context of how people project their competency in a certain domain. Psychologists David Dunning and Justin Kruger have said that people are often poor judges of their competency in a domain. The Dunning-Kruger effect is a cognitive bias whereby people with limited knowledge or competence in a specific area largely overestimate their knowledge.

I can say with reasonable confidence that one can observe the Dunning-Kruger effect at play when it comes to self-awareness. If we can treat our inner world as something that is as vast and complex and nuanced as the outer world and bring a similar curiosity to the inner world, it can be really powerful in the way we show up and the many choices we make in our journey.

At this stage, you might be asking: What is the big deal about self-awareness? What is the return on investment in it? Why now?

## Why We Should Care about Self-Awareness

Self-awareness has been a worthy pursuit of humankind for thousands of years. The Upanishadic seers of Vedic India believed that true knowledge of the 'self', and for that matter true knowledge itself could be attained only when the mind was free from the noise and distractions to which it was subject. Philosophers such as René Descartes, Plato and Socrates have pondered long and hard about existential questions that can deepen our self-awareness. 'Knowing yourself is the beginning of all wisdom,' Aristotle is known to have said. I couldn't agree more.

Let me lay out my case for why it might be a worthy pursuit to invest in self-awareness and why it is all the more critical to do it today.

*Changing leadership paradigm*: We are living in a world where the paradigm of leadership is clearly shifting from 'command and control' to 'inspire and enroll'. Given the pace of evolution in industries and technologies, I notice that leadership today is a lot more about sailing in the fog of the unknown through your humility and curiosity than driving through with authority and knowledge. A prerequisite for that, once again, is a deep understanding of who we are, what we know and more importantly what we don't know. This element becomes quite stark when I see leaders transitioning from a CXO role to a GM or a CEO/MD role. Suddenly, leaders find that there are a lot more unknowns than knowns and if they are not self-aware, I find many of them hitting a glass ceiling and stagnating in their careers.

*Reclaiming our attention*: Billions of dollars are being poured into companies like Netflix, Google and Facebook to hijack our attention. This only seems like an exponential curve as companies are engaging in an arms race to influence us and our beliefs. Instead of spending time outdoors away from our devices in nature, we find ourselves spending hours on our screens. These bits of information are coming in the way of us connecting with ourselves and lead to weakening of the tendon that connects who we are on the outside and who we are on the inside.

*Battling paradox of choice*: We are living in a world of abundance of options in every possible way. Barry Schwartz[1] says that in a world with abundant options, paradoxically enough, consumers are often less happy. While he lists multiple choices, two reasons stand out for me. Firstly, decision-making becomes complex. Secondly, people experience FOMO—Fear of Missing Out. They wonder if they should be doing something else.

Post the liberalization of 1991, the world of supply exploded in front of us. Further globalization over the years has meant that we have a plethora of options in any field, whether it is credit cards or podcasts or soap. But these are all benign use cases. The real place where this begins to make a real impact on our lives is when it comes to the world of education and careers. My father, S. Jayaraman, worked at the Indian Bank (a public sector bank) for forty years, till his demise (which came a week before his scheduled date of retirement). My father-in-law, Brigadier (Retired) V. Mahalingam, served in the Indian Army for thirty-five years and retired as a Brigadier. I am in my mid-forties, and I have worked in three organizations before starting my own practice. These days, people seem to be changing jobs every two to three years. If I look at the world of educational choices, the difference between then and now is like the difference between picking a colour from seven colours of a rainbow and picking a colour from the Asian Paints colour shade card which has about 2200 shades when I last checked! As a student graduating from Class 12 in 1993, the choices for undergraduate education were broadly along the lines of engineering, science, medicine, commerce, law, arts and social work. Most of us didn't go past option 1— engineering. Such was the aperture of our choices. Today, when I look at the various permutations and combinations of courses that people are taking, it is bewildering—psychology and law, medicine and robotics, commerce and philosophy, neuroscience and computer science, just to name a few. Please see the image below for a rough illustration of:

1) how the world of choice has changed from VIBGYOR to a shade card;
2) the number of times one must exercise choice in our journeys.

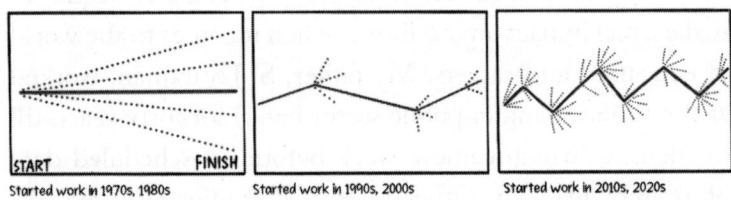

Started work in 1970s, 1980s          Started work in 1990s, 2000s          Started work in 2010s, 2020s

This explosion of aperture coupled with a dramatic increase in the number of choice points presents a very different challenge. I believe that the only way to cope with this is with heightened self-awareness. The anchor that helps us make better decisions in this world with a close to infinite supply of anything is to be very clear about who we are and what we want.

Rama Bijapurkar (🎙), a reputed board member who is also an expert in consumer behaviour, speaks about this phenomenon in the context of one particular exchange with a student from Indian Institute of Management Ahmedabad (IIMA), and how he had an abundance of career options in front of him but despite that, felt unable to move forward. Rama relates it to the conundrum that boards sometimes face in the way they deal with a company's product portfolio. She says that the more complex and volatile the world is, the more you need to understand your inner core and stay true to it.

Given the changing leadership paradigm, the criticality of reclaiming our attention and the angst that comes with the paradox of choice, self-awareness has become a must-have for us to navigate through life. A few decades back, one could argue it was nice to have. Now, if you aren't self-aware, you could be lost forever in the maze of midlife. Before we move forward, it is useful to understand an important nuance in self-awareness—the distinction between how we see ourselves and how others see us.

## Work on Internal and External Self-Awareness

I was oblivious to this distinction till my conversation with Tasha Eurich[2] (🎙), an organizational psychologist, who has studied self-awareness for several years. She categorizes it into two broad areas.

- *Internal self-awareness:* What we understand of ourselves by going inwards.
- *External self-awareness:* What the world tells us about who we are.

She goes on to say that very often working on internal and external self-awareness can reveal very different things. Her point is that the two can often be orthogonal and independent of each other.

I didn't quite comprehend the impact of it at the time she said it. But the more I seem to look around, the more instances I seem to find that validate this insight. Let me share a couple of anecdotes from my journey.

Let me start with a hobby of mine—the acoustic guitar. I have been learning it for a few years now, and I go for lessons over the weekend. Very often what I have observed is that while practising, all my effort would be on things like—1) are the notes being heard clearly?; 2) are my fingers fast enough?; and 3) am I playing to the beat? And so on. When I would practice for a week and go for my next class, the inputs would often be along the lines of a) your shoulder seems quite crouched when you play this; b) the angle of your guitar against your body is not quite right; and c) your playing is fine, but your foot tapping is off and so on. I noticed that I was so consumed in playing a tune that the kind of things I was paying attention to were very different from the kinds of things the observer (my teacher) was paying attention to. Not to say one is more important than the other. But when you combine the two views, you get a very interesting tapestry of inputs which are helpful in development and growth.

Let me share an example from the professional front. I am reminded of a conversation with Vivek Khemka, a friend and former colleague who is currently a partner at Egon Zehnder. I left the firm in 2016 and met him around 2019. I was confronted with some choices in terms of the kinds of services I should offer. Several people had also suggested that I consider expanding the team and start thinking about building a franchise given the large need that existed around transitions. As I was discussing what I do and what energizes me, Vivek stopped me in my tracks, looked me in the eye and said, 'Deepak, you seem to have an artisanal mindset.' With hindsight, I imagine he must have seen my passion for the podcast and my relative lack of interest in building a large advisory services organization. But at that stage, I found that input quite clarifying. I had not thought of myself along those lines but when he said that to me, it deeply resonated with who I thought I was and helped me make directional choices (of being a surgeon rather than building a hospital in the space I am in).

## The How of Internal Self-Awareness

In the next chapter, we will delve into the notion of external self-awareness. Let's now turn our gaze to the how of internal self-awareness—how we see ourselves. Let me outline a few practical thoughts for you to consider.

### Widen the aperture of inquiry

The quality of self-awareness, I believe, is directly linked to the kinds of reflections we have and the questions we ask ourselves. I notice that because of the common language in the feedback process in the corporate world, the default vectors of enquiry end up being strengths or development areas (what you do well, and what you could do better). The low hanging fruit in a lot of these situations is just widening the lines of inquiry.

The idea is not to turn into a philosopher and ponder over questions which may not have a material impact on the lives we lead or want to lead. The questions need to help us make sense of who we are and inform our journey. Here are ten questions that I often use with the people I coach as prompts for them to reflect. I have found them to be helpful in making sense of who we are and moving forward. Needless to say, the prompts are contextual and vary from case to case.

*In what ways have my formative years and experiences (first fifteen years) shaped me?*

I feel connecting with our childhood often has cues to how we are wired and some of our beliefs have been shaped. It gives us cues into our operating system that drives us.

*If I had to create a highlights reel of my life (like in sports) what are the few moments where I was/am at the top of my game?*

Highlight reels give us a sense of our superpowers and can help us make directional choices based on what makes us distinctive.

*What are the things I am grateful for today?*

I find that this is a useful daily prompt. I notice that several people who achieve a certain level of success often lose track of the glass 95 per cent full and focus on the 5 per cent that is empty.

*Who are the role models that inspire me?*

Sometimes, we struggle to pinpoint what we care about, and what we are striving towards. However, 'who we respect' often has clues to what matters to us. We will explore this further in chapter 5.

*What have been some of the highs and lows in the last few years?*

I find that tuning in to moments of elation and frustration can be useful navigational tool in terms of choices in our journey. These often tell us when we are in 'play' mode.

*What are some of the triggers that derail me?*

As we take on senior roles and our sphere of influence widens, I notice that while we might be composed 98 per cent of the time, the 2 per cent of the time we get triggered by something or someone, we end up doing disproportional collateral damage (given the increase in blast radius).

*When does the urgent crowd out the critical?*

This often tells us the key initiatives that are being pushed out consistently.

*How do I allocate time and attention across self/work/home/
community[3]?*

We will discuss this in greater detail in the coming chapters.
This question tests whether the way we manage our portfolio
of time and attention is consistent with what matters to us.

*What are some key choices I have made in life? How have I
thought about the trade-offs in those situations?*

Choices often tell us about what we truly value in our lives.

*What are some of the things I do, which nourish my heart and
soul?*

I notice that the corporate sector (especially in India) is
filled with people who have built their brains but have not
invested enough in nourishing their hearts. This question
pushes them to think (or rather feel) about this issue.

Needless to say, a quick Google Search will unearth
several other questions that could be used but I find these
ten to be a practical starting point to a richer picture of who
we are.

If there is one thing I have learnt (and continue to
learn) in my journey towards greater self-awareness and my
work with clients is that we need to reflect on the approach
we take in that journey. The default approach often is for
people to address it like a miner who keeps digging hard,
looking for gold or oil. However, I have empirically noticed

that we need to focus on creating the conditions of stillness and self-awareness emerges as a resultant property of that stillness. A bit like how a butterfly would come and settle on you if you sat still and dissolved into the surroundings. The paradox here, I find, is that if you go hard looking for it, then you often do not find it.

While there are many ways to pursue self-awareness (including breath work, yoga, meditation and so on), here are three practical approaches that have worked for me and some of my clients.

**Pause across timescales**

I am a big fan of the director Christopher Nolan and his movies. I love the way he deals with the concept of time in each of his movies. One of his movies, *Dunkirk*, is about the evacuation of troops from Dunkirk, a commune in France, across land, sea and air as World War II rages on. The movie shows interconnected events unfolding in three different timescales—a week (land), a day (sea) and an hour (air). I find that a similar approach is often helpful while thinking about pausing.

I request leaders I work with to consider pausing across four timescales:

a) Hourly for five to ten minutes
b) Weekly for around three hours
c) Quarterly for a day
d) Yearly for about a week

I have noticed that pausing in each timescale has a slightly different benefit and builds awareness on a different plane.

When I pause hourly, I notice that I can centre myself for the next conversation or the next activity. I see it playing the role of a thermostat, which ensures that I stay in a healthy band and do not derail, especially when I am having a bad day. I felt the value of this the most during the coronavirus pandemic. Covid hit us around mid-March 2020, and everybody around the world spent the next quarter (April–June 2020) just taking stock of what hit us and re-orienting ourselves to what was emerging. The one thing that I noticed with me and the leaders I worked with was that we had back-to-back schedules in our calendars and the offices and schools had moved into our homes. I noticed that if I wrapped up a challenging call and my children walked in to discuss something, I would get triggered and snap at them as I would typically have only a minute or two between meetings. Soon I realized that whenever I built in a ten-to-fifteen-minute buffer between meetings, I was more aware of my emotions in the moment and was able to self-regulate and catch myself from derailing more often. I have often found that when leaders pack their calendars, they end up increasing the odds of getting triggered and end up trading off effectiveness in the pursuit of efficiency. And as you rise to the top, if I had to pick one of the two, I would pick effectiveness any day.

When I pause weekly, I feel I become aware of my priorities and see if I am slipping on the key work-streams that I am supposed to pursue. I end up blocking Thursday mornings for 'me' time. I find that a week is a useful block of time for us to reflect on whether we are doing the right things or if some items are consistently slipping off the radar. If I see that some items are repeatedly not happening despite me having them on the to-do list, I often reflect on why that might be the case. Very often that has clues into what I enjoy and what I don't.

When I take a quarterly pause, I find that it gives me a sense of how I am handling the various domains of life, and how I am allocating time, attention and energy across these. Am I pouring myself too hard into work? Am I doing too much podcasting that is affecting my advisory work? Am I paying adequate attention to my health? Am I meeting friends enough or have I become too inward-focused? I find that once in three months is an appropriate frequency to take stock of the portfolio allocation across the various domains. I might have busy weeks due to the contextual spiking of one theme. But if it happens over a quarter, then I know that it possibly needs to be corrected.

When I take a yearly break (such as a solo workcation in Himachal which I took around June 2023), I find that it allows me to reflect on some of the deeper elements of purpose. I took this break in June 2023 to cover some ground on the book you are reading. But the fact that I spent time with myself in the mountains away from the din and the distractions, I felt that, over time, I developed greater conviction about my direction and the articulation around it. I find that getting this clarity requires a chain reaction of many steps but in the context switching of daily life, this chain reaction never proceeds beyond a couple of steps. An annual pause, I feel, helps us get in touch with ourselves and our direction and purpose.

These timescales are not to be taken literally but having a spread of timescales often delivers very different benefits, I have noticed. Each of us needs to adapt it to our context.

In my conversation with the chess legend Viswanathan Anand (🎤) on the podcast, he spoke about a unique dynamic that plays out around move 40 in chess. He says that when players cross move 40, they are often given a new block of time to play the next few moves. Anand speaks about how players (including him) often carry the stress of moves 37, 38, 39 and 40 into moves 41 and beyond, which ends up being counterproductive. They often do not adjust for the new block of time. He goes on to say that he developed a habit of building a pause after move 40 by going for a walk and getting some water or coffee to re-centre himself before proceeding further. We may not be playing chess at the highest level but if we think hard enough, I feel we all can find the equivalent of move 40 in our lives and build a proactive pause.

Several leaders I work with often use the car commute as an opportunity to pause and reflect and gather themselves. They ensure that they don't over-schedule themselves with too many calls in this window and just use the time to decompress and gather themselves before they get to work or return from work. That is often a sacred space where one can claim some precious 'me time' to get to the centre of the court before playing the next point.

The more we can find such opportunities in the rhythm of our lives, the easier it would be for us to sustain the practice. We discuss a few in the next section.

## Try to find mindfulness in daily life

I recognize that I am trying to provide commentary on a field where entire books have been written. Mindfulness is one such field where individuals ranging from Buddhist monks, neuroscientists to spiritual leaders have shared their wisdom over the years. I personally find it helpful to pay attention to some of the small things that I do day to day and try and find mindfulness in the rhythm of my daily life. This was an insight I picked up from Rich Fernandez.[4] This is not to say this is THE answer. While meditation, yoga and other breathing and mindfulness practices have their place, I notice that the leaders I work with are pressed for time. Hence, I find that if we can look for opportunities to channelize our attention and tune into the present in some of the daily events, the greater the odds of getting them done.

Let me share an experience in this context.

A lot of us living in India are used to outsourcing domestic activities—cleaning, cooking, sweeping and mopping—to hired house help. However, when Covid hit, this scenario changed. I added sweeping and mopping to my daily job schedule. Unlike our Western counterparts who are used to the do-it-yourself model, I guess, a lot of us in India are spoilt with these activities being taken away from our plate on a day-to-day basis. I must confess that I found the initial few days of lockdown painful and laborious. However, slowly, I tried to gamify the experience for myself. I decided to figure out how many sweeps it would take to clean the home. That led me to begin to pay attention to the number of sweeps I would do in a room and eventually in the house (I must say I never shared these ideas or statistics with my wife). I must confess that it started as an attempt to overcome boredom and distract myself. But, over a period, I noticed that when I started counting the sweeps and paying attention to each stroke, it had the effect of centering and calming me. Needless to say, when Covid subsided and our house help was back, this opportunity evaporated. But it gave me a window into how one could find mindfulness in small daily activities. The key point I want to make is that each one of us has many such opportunities to centre oneself especially when one is getting triggered. I do not claim to be doing all of the above daily. But I find that daily life is rich with opportunities to gather ourselves (beats in a song, steps during running, countdown in a traffic light, counting down or up with the elevator while waiting for it to come, ticking of the clock and so on). Pick what works for you.

**Consider developing a journaling habit**

In my role as a sounding board to leaders, the first few months are often spent driving self-awareness. While there is an element of me reaching out to the various people a leader engages with (we discuss this in the next chapter), a big chunk of the effort is often getting the leader in touch with himself/herself. I have empirically found that getting them to journal on a theme weekly or fortnightly helps them view their own iceberg very clearly. I find that when we marinate in a question, even if it is just for a few minutes every day, insights and discoveries emerge.

Rich Fernandez mentions that writing with a pen or a pencil on a sheet of paper is often more powerful than typing on a computer. He mentions that neuroscience research suggests that journaling with pen and paper almost plays the same role as running a version update on an app. We end up evolving into the next micro-version of ourselves, he says.

Here is another thought I want to share in the context of journaling. I have noticed that it is useful to decouple the process of recording something and making meaning from it. The mind, I understand, often plays tricks on us and we end up having a superficial understanding of what might be quite nuanced. I came across this wonderful insight from the management thinker Jim Collins on the *Tim Ferriss Show*.[5] Tim asked him about his journaling process, and he stated that he journals every day and notes three things in the journal (in Excel/Google Sheet):

1. Key things that happened in the day (tasks, conversations, events etc.).
2. Number of creative hours he put in (he really cares about this and has a minimum threshold of 1000 hours a year, hence he tracks this quite keenly).

3.  A number to denote how he feels about the day. He
    gives himself a whole number between -2 and +2, +2
    being a great day and -2 being a lousy day.

Jim did this for months and years and then one day decided
to make meaning of all this data. He then decided to group
all the +2s and see what was common across all those
days and similarly, grouped the -2s and see if there was a
common pattern. Even in my experience and in my work
with the people I coach, I notice that the mind is not good
at answering the 'why' in the heat of the moment. It is
good at recording the 'whats' over a period and at reflecting
on the 'why' once you have gathered sufficient data and
built sufficient distance from the moment. While I am not
as rigorous as Jim Collins, when I did this exercise for a
period of four weeks, I realized that the -2s were often days
where I had slept poorly the previous evening resulting in
me being triggered much more than other days. There is
no way I could have discovered that while journaling on
that day.

I started this journey of awareness, triggered by my
father's cancer diagnosis, in 2008. I had moved to India
from the US and was trying to make sense of what was
going on and signed up for an Art of Living course.
I subsequently did several other programmes to work
on my awareness. Thanks to this trigger, I have had an
opportunity to explore my inner world in a more sustained
and structured way over the last decade and a half. I can say
from personal experience that this exploration has given

me happiness, satisfaction and gratitude and that in turn has helped me navigate towards what I believe is my 'sweet spot' at work, build deeper and fulfilling relationships, participate in social impact and much more. I have seen that play out in the lives of my clients as well.

The point to mention here is that we are all evolving as human beings, adding and shedding layers all the time. A bit like the Ship of Theseus—a thought experiment conducted by ancient Greek philosophers. The question raised by philosophers was this: After several hundreds of years of maintenance, if each piece of the Ship of Theseus was replaced, one after the other, was it still the same ship? Like the Ship of Theseus, we keep evolving over time. Unless we pursue self-awareness as an ongoing activity, there is a high chance that we will lose touch with the latest version of the ship that is us!

Back to where we started in this chapter, in a world of abundance, our journeys look more like a maze with many twists and turns rather than a super-highway. The quality of the compass and the steering wheel begins to make a bigger and a bigger difference than the quality of the engine. That compass and steering wheel are arguably our self-awareness. If we are not intentional about our self-awareness, there is a reasonable chance that we end up as a deer frozen in front of 100 lights.

## Contextual Audio Snippets from the Podcast

- **Audio clip 3.1:** Rama Bijapurkar on the criticality of self-awareness in a world with an abundance of options and choices
- **Audio clip 3.2:** Tasha Eurich on the independence of internal and external self-awareness
- **Audio clip 3.3:** Chess legend Viswanathan Anand speaking about how he pauses around move 40, and how it helps him recenter himself
- **Audio clip 3.4:** Rich Fernandez speaks about an integrated approach to mindfulness

# WHAT LIES BENEATH

People who are highly self-aware are restless for feedback whereas people with low self-awareness already feel good about how self-aware they are

## THE PARADOX OF SELF-AWARENESS

## WHY INVEST IN SELF-AWARENESS?

Leadership paradigm is shifting from "command and control" to "Inspire and enrol"

Self-awareness is a primary prerequisite

Leadership today is about sailing in the unknown through humility & curiosity than driving through authority & knowledge

It is critical to reclaim our attention as billions of dollars are being poured to hijack it

Self-Awareness is an anchor that helps us make better decisions in a world with infinite choices

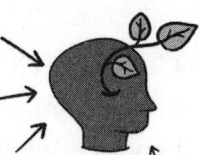

## 5 PRACTICAL IDEAS TO CULTIVATE SELF-AWARENESS

**ASK QUESTIONS BEYOND STRENGTHS AND DEVELOPMENT AREAS - WIDEN THE APERTURE OF INQUIRY FOR SELF-AWARENESS**

**LOOK AT RICHNESS OF BOTH INTERNAL AND EXTERNAL SELF-AWARENESS AND GLEAN INSIGHTS FOR OURSELVES**

**CREATE MIND-SPACE AND** PROACTIVELY BUILD A PAUSE ON DIFFERENT TIME SCALES

USE SOME OF THE DAILY EVENTS AND ACTIVITIES AS AN OPPORTUNITY TO **PAUSE AND GATHER**

**JOURNAL CONSISTENTLY TO** RUN VERSION UPGRADES ON YOURSELF

Pause

# 4

# How 360 and 365 Is Your 360

*'Feedback is the breakfast of champions'*—Ken Blanchard[1]

I have noticed that the word feedback generates a potpourri of emotions in the mind of the receiver and the giver— hope, excitement, optimism, anxiety, fear, despondence and so on.

This chapter is not about the process that companies undertake in the context of performance management, promotion and career-planning. Those are run (if at all) to solve for the company's leadership pipeline issues. In the best-case scenario, the process provides some cues on how you can do your role better, and how you can move to the next role. They are not designed to unlock your full potential as a complete human being. The corporation is not quite in the business of unlocking you! That has got to be a personal project. This chapter is about how you can be intentional about gathering insights on yourself and use those to make better choices and improve your effectiveness.

There are four dimensions around which we could be thoughtful here.

- **Where** do we go looking for insights on ourselves?
- **Who** should be gathering and interpreting the feedback?
- **What** is the nature of enquiry with the individuals that we reach out to?
- **When** and how often should we conduct this exercise?

## The Where—Look Beyond Current Colleagues

As we think about where to gather feedback, I am reminded of a story that is attributed to Nasruddin Hodja, a Persian folklore character from the thirteenth century. The story goes something like this:

*Late one evening, a man was walking home when he noticed Mullah Nasruddin on his hands and knees beneath a streetlight, carefully searching the ground. Curious, the man approached and began helping Nasruddin look for whatever he had lost. After some time, he asked where exactly the object had been dropped. Nasruddin gestured toward the darkness, indicating that it was inside his house. The man, puzzled, questioned why they were searching outside. Nasruddin simply continued his search, knowing there was more light under the streetlight than in his darkened home.*

I find that this story often captures the essence of how the feedback process plays out in several professionals' lives. We often focus on feedback (referred to as a 360 report) in our current organizations because that is where it is easily available. However, in my experience, you are met with either silence or noise, especially if you are in a position of power. Silence, because people fear to speak the truth to you. Noise because people have their agendas and are posturing to you. The real opportunity for feedback often lies elsewhere.

If we think deeper about who the various *loving critics* (people who care about us and can be constructively critical) are, that could be spoken to, three additional segments emerge:

- People outside your organization who interact with you—suppliers, customers, collaborators etc.;
- Personal relationships—spouse, siblings, parents, friends etc.; and
- Other well-wishers—former colleagues, classmates in school, mentors, mentees etc.

When we gather data from these additional constituents, we end up getting a 360-degree view and also a higher quality data set with lesser distortion and biases. We are also likely to receive useful inputs across the various domains of our life beyond work.

A related question emerges here. How do you go about seeking this data from these additional constituents? Do you do it yourself, do you get somebody else to do it for you? We will discuss this in the next section.

## The How—Get a Trusted Professional to Do It

One could argue that all it takes is to set up a Google Form (or equivalent) and send it to the people with some questions and they could give their responses (with attribution or anonymously as you prefer).

I personally feel that seeking the help of a competent professional[2] you trust can be immensely helpful for you to get the maximum value from this process. Here are the five reasons why I feel you should avoid running it as a do-it-yourself project and how you could benefit from getting another person to have these conversations and discuss them with you.

### Lack of bandwidth/mindspace

Most leaders I work with are operating at 120 per cent capacity utilization and have just about enough time for their day job. It is often hard to find the time, energy, and the mind-space to have thoughtful, reflective conversations to gather deep outside-in feedback. It is just hard to create the right mind-space for having a deep thoughtful conversation.

Roopa Kudva (🎤), who, till recently, was heading Omidyar Network in India, speaks about how she gathered outside-in feedback when she was transitioning out as the managing director of CRISIL. She had spent twenty-two years in the organization, seven of which were as the managing director and chief executive officer (CEO) of the company. When she decided to move on from CRISIL, she went on an 'outside-in' data-gathering journey that helped her meaningfully transition to the next innings. She spoke about having 'a cup of tea' with forty-five-odd people over a period of nine months during which she met policymakers, regulators or CEOs of companies and gathered feedback on what her next canvas could be. She speaks about how she first developed clarity on what she would not want to do. As she was evaluating some of the possibilities around using her skills to drive systemic change, Omidyar Network reached out to her, and she found resonance and eventually joined them.

In my experiences as a search consultant and as a transition advisor, I have noticed that people could generate the bandwidth to undertake this project of gathering outside-in data if they went on a sabbatical or if they quit their current role. But quitting is understandably risky and has a non-zero probability of the leader not finding a meaningful landing pad in good time. Even if you had the bandwidth, there are sensitivities involved in reaching out to people seeking feedback. That act itself often sets off a chain reaction that can sometimes damage the reputation of the leader. Given my empirical observations, I find the experience of Roopa Kudva more an exception than the norm. Given the sensitivities involved when you are in a role and the all-consuming nature of leadership, this exercise is often hard for a leader to embark on by themselves through their career, especially as they grow into senior roles.

## Asymmetry of power leading to silence

When leaders rise to positions of authority and influence, very often the world around them goes quiet when it comes to sharing candid feedback. People need to feel secure to be able to share their views—this is a prerequisite. Amy Edmondson (🎤), professor at Harvard Business School and one of the leading researchers in the concept of psychological safety in organizations, has spoken about the calculus people often do in their heads. The people around the leader are often weighing off a probabilistic future positive pay-off versus a certain negative pay off that could result if their opinions do not bode well with the leadership. She goes on to say that people run that calculus in their head and often, go quiet as a result due to an instinct for self-preservation. While this is often true in the context of the power structures in an organization, I have also observed in some professions, the ecosystems that an individual interacts with go quiet especially if one is positioned towards the top of the food chain. For instance, if you are a venture capitalist, it is highly unlikely that a banker or a lawyer to whom you give business will give you an honest view of how you come across. Their cash flows depend on you, and they wouldn't risk that by critiquing you.

I have noticed that when I, as a coach or as a sounding board, have these conversations and build trust with the feedback giver (internal or external) about the confidentiality and assure them of how the data will be used and how it will not impact them negatively, they often share very insightful information that is often in the blind spot of the leader or the organization.

## Awkwardness of discussing superpowers

I believe that a big element of playing to our potential is tuning into our superpowers. Things that we are distinctive at and that are unique to us. However, this data is hard to access directly from the world around us because of the awkwardness involved in the process. When was the last time you paused and pointed out somebody's superpowers?

I feel not knowing your superpower is a bigger issue than not knowing your weaknesses. I have observed that the upside of doubling down on your strengths is orders of magnitude higher than fixing your weaknesses. This is no different from how it works in the world of investing. Any venture capital investor, after he or she makes a few investments, quickly homes in on the few multi-baggers while deprioritizing the ones that are a drag to the portfolio.

In my experience, I have seen that while people may hesitate to give feedback about your superpowers directly to you, they are extremely comfortable talking about these superpowers to someone trustworthy, who collects this information on the individual's behalf. We just need a way to break through the layer of awkwardness. When I have these conversations about superpowers with my clients' inner circle, they are often effusive and very candid about their superpowers. When I debrief this with my clients, very often this is an 'aha' for them.

## Quality of inquiry

Anonymized online surveys do generate a lot of data but when you cannot contextualize it, I have noticed that people spend more time figuring out where the message came from rather than reflecting on the data.

The other challenge, which comes from online surveys, is that it is hard to decode the tonality of the message. Albert Mehrabian, professor emeritus of psychology at the University of California at Los Angeles, speaks about the 55–38–7 rule where he says that 55 per cent of the impact in any communication is body language, 38 per cent is the tonality and 7 per cent is the actual content of what is being said. If we reflect on what we gather through an online survey, we might be receiving only 7 per cent of relevant information. I don't want us to take the numbers too literally, but I hope you get a sense of how bland the output of an online survey could be.

Even if you went about gathering qualitative data as a do-it-yourself project, your ability to get the most from your conversation might be limited by your own vocabulary and worldview, and that itself could become the binding constraint in you unearthing your blind spots. Having another individual whom you trust to undertake this data-gathering expedition might help you see a more accurate and actionable picture. It is critical that this individual is competent to be able to undertake this. It is also imperative that this individual does not have vested interests in the outcome and does not project his or her biases when they return to you with the findings.

### Making sense of the excavation

This is often the last step of the meaning-making process when you conduct an outside-in feedback exercise. I have noticed that two people could look at the same situation but come up with very different conclusions. Once again, if the objective is to uncover blind spots, YOU become the binding constraint in uncovering those blind spots.

I have noticed that another skilled person could help you see the same set of data points but help you derive richer meaning from it. See image below:

Bruce Feiler (🎤), author of *Life Is in the Transitions*, uses a beautiful word 'co-narration' to describe this phenomenon. He says that when you have someone next to you, it helps to have them as an editor and co-narrate the story so that we can derive greater meaning and not be limited by our blind spots. Jennifer Garvey Berger (🎤), author of *Unlocking Leadership Mindtraps*, speaks about how our mind often settles for the simple story. Having another person help you from falling victim to this bias is effective in getting a richer insight about yourself.

In my work, I find that when I am involved in the data gathering and, in the synthesis, very often, I can see patterns that the client is blind to. A lot of the clients I work with have a 'Hanuman[3] problem'. Very often, they are not aware of their superpowers and need someone else to discern that and point it out to them. They need a Jambavan, a King of Bears. When Hanuman had self-doubt before leaping over the ocean to Lanka, Jambavan helps him get in touch with his strengths and gives him self-belief.

One of the leaders I had worked with was a managing director and chairman of the board of an auto ancillary company. He reached out to me when he was approaching retirement and wanted to be intentional about the transition. He had spent many decades in manufacturing and at some stage, he was made the managing director. It is not often that the head of manufacturing gets appointed as the managing director. Typically, it is the chief financial officer or the head of sales and marketing. He saw himself as an expert in his industry and manufacturing. When I spoke to some of his colleagues, it emerged that he was a leader who had closed many plants in the past and handled tough union situations. We discussed that this capability would be great for turnarounds and in distressed asset turnaround situations—a possibility that occurred to me but was in his blind spot. I guess that is the benefit of getting someone else to make sense of the emerging picture. When you are in a transition phase, it is often about opening new possibilities, not extrapolating the curve. Somebody who has seen different career pathways could extrapolate the same findings about you to a very different possibility in the future. Often, that is not because that person is more skilled than you. It might just be that given their aperture in life, they might have seen a different set of journeys around them. These might be in your blind spot given your mental models and lived experience.

If we are looking for insight that helps us double down on our distinctive strengths and improve our effectiveness, we need to look at the iceberg below the water surface. Our enquiry needs to be more nuanced.

## The What—Seek Beyond Strengths and Development Areas

If we really want to grow as human beings from the process of how others see us, in addition to widening the aperture of the 'who' (that we discussed in the previous section), I strongly suggest that we open the dimensions around which we gather feedback. In the previous chapter, we discussed the different ways in which we could widen the internal enquiry. I feel a similar opportunity exists when it comes to seeking feedback from the outside world.

Here are some questions that I would typically ask the respondents when I am working with a leader. What I ask whom varies depending on context.

## Some sample questions

*How did this individual get shaped by his/her childhood? What are some of the hard-wired elements of his/her personality?*

When I overlay this input against the strengths and development areas, I get a sense of the slope of change involved.

*When was this individual at his/her A-game where you felt only he/she can do that task/job?*

This often has cues around the ideal canvas where this person might flourish. This input is specifically useful if the individual is at a crossroads.

*Where has this individual changed the most/least over the last several years?*

This gives me a sense of what this person has given importance to in his or her growth journey and what are the overlooked elements of development.

*What are some of this person's superpowers that he/she may not be aware of?*

This often unearths insights which are in the blind spot of the person I am working with. People often use adjectives that are very different from what we tell ourselves.

*When does this person come alive? What brings him/her joy and meaning?*

Once we cross our mid-thirties, I have realized that it is imperative to start tuning into what we enjoy. Very often people don't discuss this. They only tell us the things we are good at, not the ones that feel like 'play' when we are in 'flow'. I have realized that we cannot work to our potential. We can only play to our potential.

*What are the principles with which this individual leads his/her life?*

This often unearths self-limiting beliefs that the person might have in terms of how they look at life. This also serves as a set of criteria which can help make more robust decisions when we are in transition.

*What is this individual after? Money/power/fame/ relationships etc.*

This is a bit like discovering where the wind is blowing; it helps me help the leader I am working with to sail towards a meaningful direction with the wind.

*If you had a blank canvas, what is the space where this individual could really flourish over the next several years?*

I find that people are often reactive when they get to positions of power and authority; they respond to opportunities that come their way (through search consultants and otherwise); looking at the individualities of a leader and starting with a blank canvas can sometimes catalyze new possibilities.

*How does the person prioritize across self, family, work and community? What could he/she do more of or less of?*

I notice that very often people in one domain give feedback in that domain. Our family looks at how we are as a parent/child/sibling/spouse. Our work colleagues look at how well we do at work. It is helpful to have a portfolio view of how we are dealing with life and where we might be under-indexing or overinvesting.

*What might be in the blind spot of the individual? Something that you see but the individual may not notice or acknowledge?*

This often throws up a really nuanced insight or two which often takes my client by surprise.

This is just a sample indicative list. However, I hope this gives you a sense of how shallow and limiting the traditional workplace feedback can be in the context of gathering outside-in intel on yourself. That process is not designed to unlock the best version of YOU! The only way to enable that is to take charge of this for yourself and take this as a personal project rather than be subject to the vagaries of an annual process that the company runs.

## The When—Go Beyond Once in 365 Days

I am a big believer in taking ownership of seeking regular feedback as a way of life. It doesn't have to be a once-in-a-year kind of exercise. If we are thoughtful and proactive enough, we can create a drip feed of outside-in feedback which can help us become better versions of ourselves.

I have been in advisory services all my life across consulting, executive search and coaching, and I have found it incredibly helpful to adopt the mindset of a customer-facing professional from the hospitality industry—being obsessed about how a guest perceives the experience and tuning into the minutest of emotions they might display.

There are many moments when we can pause and gather feedback from the other person. Let me illustrate one. This was something I learnt when I was at Egon Zehnder from my mentor, Govind Iyer. I had just started working on a search with a client where I had to find the country head for a logistics business. I was deep in work when one day Govind walked in and asked me, 'What does the client want from this search?' I was a little perplexed. I told him that they were looking at getting a candidate for the role that was vacant. Clearly, I didn't get the point. Govind repeated the question and after a few rounds of back and forth went on to explain that while a search is a search is a search, each context is different. Some clients are looking to leverage Egon Zehnder branding to access a certain pool of candidates, some clients are looking for help with Board Management in the context of a hire, some are looking for global outreach and so on. The late Clay Christiansen[4] uses the phrase 'jobs to be done' to describe it. What is it that people 'really' want when they hire us? When we try and discern that at the outset, it also throws light on how people see us and what specific value they seek from us.

I try and do that whenever I start a new relationship with a client. '*Why me?*', however narcissistic or self-congratulatory it sounds, opens the door to many insights, I notice. I have come to understand that what is 'value' can be different for different people in different contexts and unless we explicitly seek feedback, we will never know.

While there is tremendous value in being proactive about gathering feedback as we go through our journeys, I notice that some of the most valuable feedback comes our way when we least anticipate it. It may not come to us packaged as feedback. It might be a passing comment in a conversation or a snap observation somebody makes momentarily. Very often, I notice that it is just a case of slowing down the tape and creating the space for tuning into those whispers.

Anu Madgavkar (🎤), partner at McKinsey Global Institute, speaks about how, in a job interview, a question asked by an interviewer led to a cascade of reflections, providing her clarity on who she was and showed her the kind of canvas on which she might flourish. She speaks about how the interviewer pointed out that she wasn't happy in one of her stints and as she thought further about it, she discovered that it was possibly because she was collaborative as a person and that situation demanded a certain level of competitive behaviour that didn't come naturally to her. All of us have these moments where we have people showing the mirror to us, only if we pause more to pay attention and process what we are being told!

If I look at the last fifteen-odd years of my life, a couple of spontaneous 'outside-in' perspectives have fundamentally changed the course of my journey.

The first was around 2009 from Ramesh Mangaleswaran, who at that time was a senior partner at McKinsey in the Chennai office. When I was evaluating career pathways post-McKinsey, I was initially looking at traditional options such as strategic planning roles, venture capital, private equity etc. I remember Ramesh looking me in the eye and telling me that I had a strong people orientation, and I should consider a career in executive search. He went on to introduce me to the team at Egon Zehnder which has led me to where I am today. If not for that 'outside-in' view, this possibility may not have come to life.

The second came around 2014 when I was at Egon Zehnder. I was about three years into the firm. I had made principal (a milestone to indicate that one is on the path to partnership). However, I was middling in my performance in the firm and wasn't also having a lot of fun doing the work. I was enjoying the career counselling conversations with candidates more than the evaluative conversations in the context of a role. When I joined the Egon Zehnder, some of my mentors mentioned that search, in a lot of ways, was like strategy consulting. You solve tough ambiguous problems, you must be creative about your approach, and you engage with clients on their most critical issues. What I discovered along the way was that while the front end of the search felt like consulting, the back end felt like investment banking. The phase when you are trying to hustle and 'close the deal'. It is an art and some people do it well. I didn't have the will or the skill to do it. When I was discussing how I felt about my journey with a close friend, he looked at me and said, 'You seem to have more of a coaching mindset than a poaching mindset.' It was spontaneous but I found it to be such a pithy synthesis of the dissonance I was facing at the level of mindset, not skill set. In a way, that was the input that set off a series of actions that have led me to where I am today.

These just happen to be two conversations that I can recount at the top of my mind. I am sure there are many that I have failed to tune into. I have come to realize the value of creating the space to reflect on the various whispers that come our way, and as you would recognize, it is a journey. If we create adequate stillness and space in our relationships, I find that people tell us things in a low volume that can be extremely valuable in the way we navigate our lives.

## Case Study—Feedback as a Drip Feed

One of my clients is the general partner of a venture capital fund. I play the role of a coach/sounding board for him in the context of his professional and personal journey. We have been on this coaching journey for close to three years (and counting) where we have agreed that I will speak to different clusters of people and share with him the various perspectives as a 'drip feed'.

- **Wave 1:** Spouse, sister, mother, current co-founders and current colleagues.[5]
- **Wave 2:** Past colleagues in the two organizations he had worked in (McKinsey and another venture capital fund) and some close childhood friends.
- **Wave 3:** Entrepreneurs that he has invested behind and had a strong exit.
- **Wave 4:** Limited partners who invest in his fund.
- **Wave 5:** Some of the bankers and lawyers who have worked closely with him on his deals.
- **Wave 6:** Entrepreneurs where one of his partners is on the board (to discern how he is seen as adding value in those situations where he is not the primary investor).
- **Wave 7:** Individuals to whom he is a mentor.

Each wave lasts about a quarter. We process the feedback, discuss the implications for the individual and keep moving forward. Every now and then, I would go back to the people from a certain wave and discuss how the leader has moved on a certain trajectory to see how the transformation is coming along. Each vantage point offers a unique perspective. For instance, in Wave 6, it emerged that my client was turning out to be a great cheerleader for the entrepreneurs and truly cared about their health and well-being. The entrepreneurs really valued the human touch and empathy that my client brought to the relationship, something that was a rarity in the venture capital circles. It was something that came as a pleasant surprise, and it has helped him to double down on those behaviours in the situations he was involved in. What we think is value and how people perceive value could be very different things. If we don't ask, we will never know.

When you overlay the insights you receive from this process with the insights from the internal voyaging (as discussed in the earlier chapter), you end up with a rich, high-definition picture that helps you see yourself clearly and walk the journey with intent and conviction.

When we are going through a transition phase, it is crucial for us to tune into some of the deeper elements of who we are. This includes our fears, beliefs, values, principles and many other elements which sometimes are hard to access through the methods we have discussed in the last couple of chapters. We look at some of the deep excavation techniques in the next chapter.

## Contextual Audio Snippets from the Podcast

- **Audio Clip 4.1:** Roopa Kudva speaks about how she took outside-in feedback when she transitioned out of CRISIL.
- **Audio Clip 4.2:** Prof. Amy Edmondson (of Harvard Business School) speaks about the Calculus of Silence that people run in their heads before choosing to speak.
- **Audio Clip 4.3:** Bruce Feiler discusses the benefits of co-narrating a story with another person.
- **Audio Clip 4.4:** Jennifer Garvey Berger discusses how humans have the ability to often settle for a simple story.
- **Audio Clip 4.5:** Anu Madgavkar speaks about a moment of epiphany in an interview process.

# HOW 360 and 365 is your 360

## TO GET MOST VALUE FROM OUTSIDE-IN FEEDBACK, BE THOUGHTFUL ABOUT:

### WHO

Take advantage of a Trusted Advisor and do a high-touch (rather than online) to seek rich actionable data

### WHERE

Reach out to diverse 'loving critics' who have a perspective on you from various domains of life (professional/personal)

Actions
Behaviour
Strengths
Results
Development Areas
Start/Stop/Continue

**THE ICEBERG OF SELF-AWARENESS**

PERSONAL EVOLUTION

INDIVIDUAL SUPERPOWERS

INNATE TALENT

LIFE EXPERIENCES

WHAT GIVES JOY & MEANING

HARD WIRING

### WHAT

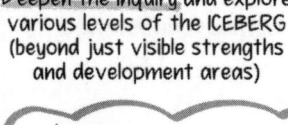

Deepen the inquiry and explore various levels of the ICEBERG (beyond just visible strengths and development areas)

### WHEN

Gather feedback as 'drip feed' along the journey rather than doing it annually. Create stillness and space to process the feedback that come your way

OVERLAY INSIGHTS FROM GAINING EXTERNAL SELF-AWARENESS WITH INTERNAL SELF-AWARENESS AND YOU HAVE A RICH, HIGH-DEFINITION PICTURE THAT HELPS YOU SEE YOURSELF CLEARLY

# 5

# Tuning into Our Values and Principles

*Kisi ki muskurahaton pe ho nisaar*
*Kisi ka dard mil sake to le udhaar*
*Kisi ke vaste ho tere dil mein pyaar*
*Jeena isika naam hai*

Offer yourself to bring a smile to someone
If you can, offer your shoulder to bear someone's pain
Have love for someone in your heart
This is what life is about

—Lyrics: Shailendra;
movie: *Anari*; singer: Mukesh

An adult makes about 30,000 conscious decisions each day[1] regarding various elements of his/her life. This boils down to a decision every two to three seconds. This includes decisions around how we spend our time and attention across the various domains of our life. Without getting bogged down by the specifics, let us just say that the number runs into thousands. These accumulated choices come together over a lifetime to lead us to varying outcomes. These choices impact not just us but often create a ripple effect for our families, teams, businesses, communities and beyond. If you think the numbers are staggering at a daily level, when we look at a prolonged block of time stretching into years, these choices compound and impact the eventual tangible and intangible balance sheet of us and the people around us.

I believe playing to our full potential requires us to deliberately scale a few compounding curves and that compounding is unlikely to happen if there is no governing framework for all these thousands of decisions we make along the way. I believe that the underlying governing framework that helps us make these micro-choices is our set of values.

A lot of us are familiar with values in the context of organizations. For instance, Johnson & Johnson has a document called the Credo[2] that was crafted in 1943, and it still acts as the document that guides the various actions of the company. Credo outlines the various stakeholders to whom the employees are accountable and urges them to make sustainable and inclusive profits rather than maximizing profits at all costs. Apart from providing decision-making clarity, they also help in signalling. When you share your values publicly, they help the people around you to know why you do what you do and help build trust and attract your tribe over time.

I have noticed that if we can be intentional about our values and tune into them, it can help us make coherent[3] decisions across time and the various domains of our lives and that consistency and slow compounding will help us play to our full potential.

These are the four values with which I strive to live my life. Needless to say, they might evolve with time, but this is where they stand now.

***Help people play to their unique and full potential:*** I try and hold myself accountable to this across the various interactions I have, not just the clients I serve. I believe that one of the elements of playing to potential is a lot about shaping the playground we operate in (a topic we will discuss later in the book). Wherever relevant, I try and proactively share feedback and observations with people about their natural wiring and the canvas they are likely to flourish on. This has also got me to focus on unlocking the full potential of an individual as a whole rather than just focusing on the work persona. This means that in the work I do, I strive to engage with the personal and professional ecosystems that the leader engages in for me to form a full view which helps me nudge them towards leading a full life beyond work.

***Bring an artisanal mindset to the work I do:*** *Jiro Dreams of Sushi* is a documentary film released in 2011, directed by David Gelb. The movie centres on Jiro Ono, an octogenarian chef who is considered one of the world's greatest sushi chefs, and owns a renowned restaurant, Sukiyabashi Jiro, a modest establishment located in a Tokyo subway station that has earned three Michelin Stars for its exquisite sushi. The crux of the film lies in its exploration of Jiro Ono's relentless pursuit of perfection in sushi-making, his unwavering dedication to his craft, and the discipline and hard work that underpin his success. It showcases the beauty of simplicity in cuisine, the importance of traditional methods, and the dedication required to achieve greatness. The movie is inspiring, demonstrating how a life's work can be an art form.

Jiro Ono is a personal hero of mine, and I try and bring an artisanal approach to the work I do. For instance, in the *Play to Potential* podcast, we break down a conversation into smaller pieces (that we call nuggets), and then I try and come in with my thoughts on the topic or cross-reference an insight with something that has been said in a different conversation. The nuggets are also tagged by theme so that listeners can peruse multiple voices on a topic they are curious about. All this requires painstaking work, and many people ask me if it is worth it. But I enjoy doing it as it allows me to reflect deeply about the content I am creating and hopefully, the value of the library[4] as a collective web of wisdom is much more than the sum of its parts.

***Strive for a sense of balance across various pursuits:*** I have discovered that I am generally at my best when I operate from a sense of balance and harmony across the various

domains of life rather than when I am going all guns
blazing in one area. The things that matter to me outside
of work include time with my family, time for exercise, the
opportunity to learn and play the guitar and some element
of philanthropy. When I try and slot these big rocks into
my bowl, I notice that there is often not a lot of time for
other demands such as playing a cricket league (a sport that
I am passionate about), socializing with second-degree
connections, taking on assignments beyond a certain
threshold etc. I have come to realize that time is finite and
unless we have a well-articulated set of values for ourselves
and others, it is easy to be spread thin and feel a certain
sense of misery that comes from time poverty. I find that
we all need to say yes to three things and no to hundreds of
things, and values help in doing that.

***Spend as much time as possible in the state of PLAY:*** I have
come to realize that each one of us cannot work to our
full potential. We can only play to our potential. This has
helped me move away from profitable work that feels like
'work' more than 'play'. When I set out on my journey as
an independent consultant after Egon Zehnder, I started
doing different pieces of work that were broadly in the
realm of enhancing leadership. This included some work
with leadership teams as a group including facilitating
offsites to improve 'top team effectiveness'. As I did a few
of those, I realized that while having a deep one-on-one
conversation with a leader came naturally to me, working
with a group felt laborious. I also felt that I was not being

effective in those situations. Today, I try not to work in situations where I am expected to move a group as a collective in a certain direction.

While these were ideas that were in my head earlier, I have started evaluating my 'why' every now and then and publicly sharing it on LinkedIn and other platforms so that people can hold me accountable as I undertake my journey. I also recognize that this is not a static thing. As my life context evolves, my experiences shape me and what I discover about myself, my values will evolve. But I have noticed that stating it explicitly for ourselves and the people around us can provide decision-making clarity and allow us to compound in a few domains that we care about—whether it is our professional pursuits or relationships that we care about or our health.

The question that arises next is how one discovers or shapes these values. I have observed that values often must be excavated from deep within. There are three approaches I would like to share in this context that I have seen working.

1. Make sense of your regrets.
2. Use role models to infer your values.
3. Tune into reflections around life-quakes.

As you would appreciate, tuning into our values is not a predictable, linear process. I have noticed that when we combine our insights gleaned from gathering internal and external self-awareness with these three, one can often get to a coherent set of values which can act as a lighthouse when we are stranded on the high seas and help us with the micro-choices that move us forward in our lives.

## Make Sense of Your Regrets

In 2011, Bronnie Ware, a palliative nurse, published her book, *The Top 5 Regrets of the Dying*. Given the profession she was in, she had a unique lens on the lives of the dying as she moved from individual to individual while they lived out their last few days.

She outlined the following regrets as the ones that the people on their deathbed spoke about.

1. I wish I'd had the courage to live a life true to myself, not the life others expected of me to;
2. I wish I hadn't worked so hard;
3. I wish I had the courage to express my feelings;
4. I wish I had stayed in touch with my friends; and
5. I wish I had let myself be happier.

Research also suggests that towards the end of life, people regret their omissions much more than their commissions. For a long time in my life, I used to believe that having no regrets was a good way to live a meaningful life. That was until I had an opportunity to speak to Dan Pink[5] (🎤), the author of *The Power of Regret* who speaks about regret as a useful vehicle to understand what we truly value. He calls it the photographic negative of the life that we all would want to live. While we don't have to wait for us to arrive at our deathbeds to tune into this, the loss of a loved one and looking at their lives closely can help us get in touch with our regrets.

After speaking to Dan, I discovered that I regretted not having done further research in the form of a PhD. This was around 2004, and I had completed about five years of work as a management consultant. There was an itch to study more and go deeper into a subject. There was also a desire to pursue a globally recognized degree as a jumpstart into a global career.

I started exploring potential programmes at that stage and was initially tempted to do a PhD, but the people around me advised that if I wanted to return to a career in the corporate world, a PhD was the wrong pathway. Instead, they nudged me towards pursuing an MBA from a top global school. What I did not realize at that time was that these advisers were projecting their aspirations and guiding me based on what they thought would have been right for them if they were in my shoes. It was not necessarily what was right for me given my vision for my future. I did not quite appreciate this nuance then.

A few months back, one of the podcast listeners kindly wrote to me that she liked listening to the *Play to Potential* podcast. When I asked her for feedback on what she liked about the podcast, she mentioned that she felt that I had a research mindset (rather than a marketing mindset) in the way I conducted and curated the *Play to Potential* podcast and that made it a worthwhile experience for her as a consumer of the content. It struck me that when I had decided to pursue the path of an independent consultant, I wanted to become a lifelong student of leadership, transitions and careers and in a way that was the genesis of the *Play to Potential* podcast. Not doing a PhD was a regret of mine for a long time. Tuning into this regret has helped me channel it into a podcast and the book that you are reading now. One could argue this is post-facto rationalization but connecting the dots here has helped me become more intentional about differentiating the podcast from the rest of the content out there by bringing a researcher's mindset rather than a marketer's mindset to the work I do.

## Use Role Models to Infer Your Values

Tuning into who we admire and deducing some of the themes around it can also shine a light on our values. This is something I learnt from my podcast conversation with Rama Bijapurkar, an independent board member in many blue chip companies and one of the leading thinkers in the areas of marketing, market research and the Indian consumer behaviour. She speaks about how one of her friends urged her to think about three role models who influenced her, and how through that she deduced what she valued. Rama mentions that when she thought about her role models, it turned out to be a list of three which included a leading strategy guru, a famous lawyer and a singing maestro. She went on to speak about how that shaped her career choices as an independent director, business advisor, 'people' researcher and author.

After my conversation with Rama, I have been reflecting on who my role models are and how they have shaped my values. When I did this exercise recently, I noticed that I had three very different kinds of people on my list. But when I tried to connect the dots across these three, some common patterns emerged.

- *Sir David Attenborough:* I love the way David has been committed to nature conservation for an entire lifetime. His filmography as writer, presenter and narrator has spanned eight long decades. I find it incredible that somebody committed such a long time to one cause and really kept at it. A fascinating statistic is that he is the only person to have won BAFTA awards for programmes in black and white, colour, high-definition, 3D and 4K. Talk about evolving with the times. I remember watching his latest production on Netflix, *A Life on Our Planet: My Witness Statement and a Vision for the Future* (2020). It was truly inspiring to see an individual in his nineties, passionately pursuing his craft and doing his bit to move the planet in the right direction.
- *Alexander Babu:* Alexander (Alex) is a renowned stand-up comedian from Tamil Nadu. He speaks about his journey as a software engineer in the US, how he got frustrated with it, returned to India and found his calling as a stand-up comedian. I also love the way he has married his passion and talent in music and woven

it very cleverly into his performances. Like a lot of people, including me, who grew up in the south in the eighties and nineties, Alex is a big fan of Ilayaraja (the music composer) and features a lot of that material in his comedy. One of the pieces of advice that one receives is that we all should shape our own unique playgrounds. I love the way Alex has been able to bring his unique set of strengths and context (knowledge in music, humour, early roots in small towns in Tamil Nadu) to bear and carve out a unique career for himself.

- *Robin Williams's character in* Good Will Hunting:[6] Robin Williams plays Dr Sean Maguire, a teacher of psychology and a therapist. He is entrusted to work with Will Hunting (played by Matt Damon) who is a gifted genius but is leading a carefree life. One of the professors at MIT notices his gift and wants to channel his talent towards solving more complex problems and seeks Sean's help in channelling Will. The backbone of the movie is about the dynamic between Sean and Will, and how they transform each other through that journey. When I look back, I would say that might have been the first time a seed was planted in my head that I wanted to be in the profession of helping people find their potential. I do not think that I even paid attention to it, but it was one of those whispers that I never listened to at that time in my life.

Looking at Sir David gives me the conviction to stay true to a topic for a prolonged period of time and see what I am doing as a multi-decadal pursuit. Staying committed to the field of nature conservation has given him a nuanced sense of the issues and challenges around preserving the planet. It has also helped millions of people build trust with him and to be inspired by him. Observing him going about his craft gives me hope that staying true to the theme of unlocking one's full potential and creating purposeful content would be of long-term value. It feels like I have only taken baby steps in that direction. Moving to Alex, I notice that he is around my age and perhaps one of the reasons I find him a role model is that he decided to go solo at a similar time as I chose to walk away from the corporate treadmill. I admire the way he shapes his playground by creating a brand of humour that celebrates his uniqueness. His shows are filled with references to '80s and '90s music. As a trained musician, he often breaks into a performance and that combination of music and humour is quite unique. I am not sure if he would have been as successful if he had just been another comedian trying to fit himself into a standard template. When I look at my journey, I realize that I have a unique set of skills given my background in management consulting, executive search and personal transformation. In my work, I strive not to fit what I do into what might be defined as a 'templatized coaching process'. I realize that it doesn't quite bring out what is unique about me. Finally, having Sean Maguire as a role model pushes me to live a balanced life (like he does) and not fall victim to the 'rat race' that his classmate (the character of Professor Gerald Lambeau) is on. Finally, I notice that all three are not really leaders of corporations but artisans in their respective domains who are using their craft to make a difference.

Reflecting on who our role models are and what about them inspires us can help connect us with our values.

## Make Meaning from Life-Quakes

I was introduced to the term life-quake by Bruce Feiler (🎤), author of the book *Life Is in the Transitions*. He defines life-quakes as those few events in our life that really shake us to our core and get us to examine our beliefs about ourselves and the world around us. Events like divorce, a health crisis, the loss of a loved one or a sudden layoff can shake us to the core and disorient us. Covid-19 was a life-quake that we all experienced concurrently.

Life-quakes often present an interesting opportunity for us to get in touch with our values and to rethink and reimagine our lives. I experienced one such event in 2008. While Lehman Brothers went bankrupt in 2008, and the financial and the business worlds were dealing with the tremors from that quake, I had a different one going on in my personal life.

### Losing my father

I lost my father to stage IV colon cancer in 2008. I was pursuing a career with McKinsey US then and was looking to build a career there. However, when my father was diagnosed with cancer, my wife and I moved back to India to take care of his treatment. Given my context, McKinsey[7] was kind enough to temporarily relocate me from New Jersey to Chennai. In those six months that transpired between his diagnosis in March 2008 and his passing away in October 2008, I discovered a thing or two about values.

Stage IV cancer is a unique social experiment that Mother Nature conducts. It is one of those few conditions where you get an opportunity to see people transition from living an open-ended life to being part of a countdown (with unpredictable duration). It seems like suddenly these individuals have been given a pair of binoculars with which they can see the finish line and work their way back from it. I could see my father shift from a current plus life to a future minus life. While I didn't realize it at that time, those six months of seeing my father live life with a ticking clock taught me a thing or two about the importance of using death to tune into one's values.

In those six months, I saw him change in many different ways as he moved to life with a countdown clock. Three things stood out for me.

I saw him develop gratitude for the smallest of things that we would take for granted. For instance, I remember a day when he was undergoing his fourth round of chemotherapy. It was around July, about a quarter after his diagnosis. His digestive system would take a beating each time he would go through a chemo session. While we were being extremely measured with his diet given his fragile digestive system, on one of the evenings, he decided to indulge his taste buds and dig into his favourite meal of onion sambhar with roasted potato—a delicacy among South Indian vegetarians. We all waited with bated breath the next morning to check if he was able to pass stool without discomfort. When he came out and gave us a thumbs up, the household erupted into a mini celebration. I saw him develop gratitude for mini moments that brought him joy in an otherwise gloomy situation.

The second element I saw change was that he started paying attention to the few relationships that mattered to him and cut out the noise in terms of cursory pleasant acquaintances that would often take up disproportionate time in his day-to-day existence. I saw my father make time for people who came and spent time with him and had positive conversations. I could see that while he enjoyed the warmth of the near and dear family, he experienced true joy when some of his close friends who came home to visit him and regaled him with silly stories from the past. I noticed that family couldn't quite replace some of these multi-decadal relationships that he had. I remember that during those days, one of the people who visited our home was the chairman and managing director (CMD) of the public sector bank where my father spent more than forty years of his life. My father was part of the middle-management in the bank. Six months earlier, the CMD of the bank visiting our home would have been a big deal for him. While he was grateful that the leader of the bank visited him, I could see that it didn't do anything emotionally for my father. The same evening, one of his friends who had played cricket with him since childhood showed up, and I could see my father really relishing the company and reminiscing about the conversation for the next few days. It told me something about the connections we form at work and true life-long relationships.

Thirdly, I saw my father slowly but surely starting to prepare for the eventual transition. He was the treasurer of the Residents' Association of the building in Chennai where my parents lived. He ensured a complete handover of the various accounts and tallied the accounts till the last rupee as he handed over the charge. I could see him become deliberate about bringing my sister and me into the loop when it came to his finances so that my mother and us had full visibility of the investments he had made.

While my father went through a lot of pain and suffering, it gave me a glimpse into how joyful and meaningful life could be if we could bring that 'endgame' mindset into our daily lives. In a way that passage of play got me to reflect deeply about who I was and what mattered to me and was the catalyst from my journey as a McKinsey consultant in the US to what I do now.

### Losing a shining star—Amit Bordia

Sometimes, we see people around us deal with life-quakes and how they think about life can sometimes be immensely clarifying. I had this experience when I lost my friend and classmate from IIMA, Amit Bordia, to cancer in 2023. He was diagnosed with bone marrow cancer out of the blue in 2019, and then went on to live out the next four years battling several probabilities and procedures.

Amit was a force of nature and somebody who had the rare gift of great intellect coupled with extraordinary interpersonal skills, negotiation capability, political savviness, stage presence, ambition and more. He was the gold medallist of the 1999 IIMA batch. One of our friends summed up his personality by way of a dialogue which Shah Rukh Khan uses in the movie *Raees*: '*Baniye ka dimaag aur miya bhai ki daring* [The brains of a Baniya and the courage of a miyaan]![8] He had a successful run as a banker at Deutsche Bank and was starting as an entrepreneur in 2018 when he got diagnosed with cancer. In the four-plus years, he went through various ups and downs including failed bone marrow transplants. He even got Covid in the middle of all this and fought his way through it. He breathed his last on 1 March 2023. A valuable life that ended too soon.

Among the things he left behind, one of the treasures was his note to his IIT Delhi classmates in the context of his not being able to attend the twenty-five-year reunion in December 2022.

### Reflection from Amit Bordia[9]

*Doston*, I have seen how life can turn 180 degrees within hours; have been battling low survival probabilities for the last four years and have seen the important become mundane and the ignored become omnipresent—I cannot help but share some reflections from that.

We often seem to get happy or sad based on how daily events and people's reactions pan out. What my boss thought of my email, did a friend return my call, did a family member wish me on my birthday, a profile raise or a work opportunity materializing, a small gain in investment returns—all this seem to matter a lot. If we plotted happiness on the Y-axis and time on the X-axis, I realized that for most of the years, I had been shooting for what turned out to be small local maxima and getting very upset about hitting small local minima. And then one day, the baseline moved! And what was all-consuming started seeming utterly meaningless, irrelevant and unbelievably naive for me to have spent all my energies on, while I had them.

So please focus on securing the baseline—or at least keep watching it. I believe that health (own and of those close to you), financial security for the family, or decay in relationships can all move the baseline dramatically—each of these has the potential to permanently take a chunk of joy out of living and thereby rendering the local maxima we were chasing a waste. Do cherish and nurture your relationships and experiences and memories—those are all I have had in numerous nights spent on my hospital bed.

Would also recommend giving to others when you can—share your love, effort, wealth, happiness and attitude. A small plug—I have now twice received stem cells for my transplants from completely voluntary strangers—people whom I still don't know but might end up saving my life. Please look up opportunities to register for stem cell donations—there is a global registry with a lot of local centres—all it takes to register is a cheek swab, the donation is completely regenerative and harmless, the probability of being called is very low but the contribution to someone's life could be immense. Please also encourage your kids (16+) to look into this.

And to the basics please—get regular health check-ups, even if no symptoms—that's how I was diagnosed—and DO not ignore if anything is out of range (there is always a reason the ranges are large). Do have generous health and life insurance figured and prepare a will.

I have seen enormous support pour out of our IIT community and feel secure in the knowledge that if I need help of any kind, I have you rooting for me. And I would simply be incapable of mounting this fight without the support of those I forged such close bonds with on campus.

I hope to bounce back—but meanwhile just wanted all of you to know that spending time at IIT-Delhi and with you all has been the greatest privilege and the most enriching experience of my life and for that, I will be eternally grateful.

I found two things immensely clarifying in Amit's note. Firstly, it shone the light on how we end up fretting over local optima while they pale in significance to wider tectonic shifts. Secondly, he speaks about the three things—health, relationships and money—that can significantly move our baseline, and how we need to watch it like a hawk.

As we go through our journeys, I find that there is a lot of noise around what matters, and what we should focus on. This has been further amplified by social media and democratization of publishing. However, when we or somebody else around us goes through a life-quake, it can be an opportunity for us to have another look at our values.

I should mention that there is something about the timing of the reflection when we or someone around us is going through a life-quake. We need to ensure that we do not do it when the wounds are raw. We are likely to get to a better place if we wait for some time to elapse before we start making sense of what we have experienced. Once some time elapses and wounds become scars, it becomes more productive to engage in this reflection. Ramesh Srinivasan[10] (🎤) speaks about the pain and trauma that he and his wife Charuta Joshi went through when they lost both their children to cancer. Their daughter, Shruti, was nine years old when she passed away in 2009. Their son, Aditya, was almost twelve when he passed away in 2015. Ramesh speaks about the criticality of going through a phase of recovery before moving to a phase of re-imagination. These days, Ramesh and Charuta channel their energy and spend some time with several education centric-profits and other institutions and make a difference to millions of children.

There are many ways in which we can tune into our values/principles. These just happen to be three of the approaches that have worked for me. Being intentional and doing the work to clearly articulate what these are for you can give you navigational clarity as you deal with the various micro and macro-choices that you have to make in your life.

* * *

Section B was about doing the inner work for us to get in touch with ourselves. Nuanced self-awareness is a must-have for us to engage with the approach that is laid out in the upcoming chapters in Section C. Each one of us is unique in a very special way and is on a bespoke journey. The more we recognize this, greater the odds of crafting a life that is fit for purpose to who we are and what we seek!

## Contextual Audio Snippets from the Podcast

- **Audio Clip 5.1:** Dan Pink on regret: The photographic negative of the life we want to lead
- **Audio Clip 5.2:** Bruce Feiler on life-quakes: How we can derive meaning from them
- **Audio Clip 5.3:** Ramesh Srinivasan on recovery and re-imagination phase during a life-quake

# TUNING INTO OUR VALUES AND PRINCIPLES

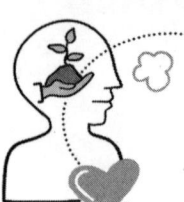

In the world of abundant choices, personal values can :

💚 Guide your choices

💚 Help you live a life in congruence with who you are

**Values are buried deep within and hard to excavate**

## THREE APPROACHES TO GAIN CLARITY ON OUR VALUES

IF ONLY...

### MAKE SENSE OF YOUR REGRETS

We regret our omissions more than our commissions

Regret is a useful vehicle to understand what we truly value

### USE ROLE-MODELS TO INFER YOUR VALUES

Reflecting on who our role models are and what about them inspires us can help us connect with our values

### MAKE MEANING FROM LIFE-QUAKES

Events that shake us or people around us can help us get in touch with what really matters and what we truly value

# SECTION C

 THE LONG AND MESSY MIDLIFE

 GETTING IN TOUCH WITH OURSELVES

 **AN APPROACH TO A FULL LIFE**

# 6

# Crafting a FLAVOUR-ful Life

*Another turning point, a fork stuck in the road*
*Time grabs you by the wrist, directs you where to go*
*So make the best of this test, and don't ask why*
*It's not a question, but a lesson learned in time*
*It's something unpredictable*
*But in the end, it's right*
*I hope you had the time of your life*
                    —'Good Riddance' by Green Day

When I worked as a search consultant at Egon Zehnder, I was on the lookout for individuals who were outstanding professionals. That is what clients paid us for. To separate the wheat from the chaff. Our primary lens was to look at individuals who could be a good fit for the organization and add significant commercial value to the enterprise. However, since 2016, in my role as a coach and as a podcaster, I have been on the lookout for individuals who seem to be striving to play to their full potential given the context they are in. These are people who seem happy and fulfilled in real life (not just in their Facebook, Instagram and WhatsApp photos). These people are healthy and have thriving relationships around them. They seem to be highly aware of their life-situation and make choices which seem to be contextually appropriate. They seem to be doing justice to their various roles (as a parent, spouse, sibling, professional, member of the community and more) and leading a full life. It is not that their life is all hunky-dory and all moments are perfect. These individuals have their share of challenges thrown at them, but they seem to have the ability to navigate their life with a certain sense of clarity, grace and equanimity. They may not necessarily be operating in the sweet spot of ikigai but still, I would like to believe, are striving to play to their full potential in the context they are in and under the constraints they are faced with. Not all these people are the kinds of people that might appear in newspapers and magazines, but we all come across these role models around us who show us what leading a full life might entail. To put it differently, we are all dealt with a certain set of cards in life. The real question to ask is: Are we doing the best we can, given the cards we are dealt with as we undertake our journey? The rest of the book is about trying to decode what some of these people might be doing (even though they might be doing it intuitively).

There are more than eight billion people around the world leading very uniquely different lives. However, when

I look at some of these diverse sets of people playing to their full potential, there seems to be a convergence of a few themes that I wanted to present to you as an emerging hypothesis. I hope it provides you with language as you take stock of life and make choices and seek to play to your full potential. In the coming years, I will strive to collect further data to sharpen this thinking further.

In the rest of this chapter, we will look at the FLAVOUR framework that I believe might help you play to your full potential. In Chapter 7, we will look at six diverse journeys (three women and three men) and look at how they have strived to play to their full potential as life has unfolded for them. In Chapter 8, we look at some of the meta-skills that might be required for us to play to our full potential as we journey through life. Finally, in Chapter 9, we look at how we could go about rediscovering our FLAVOUR as we go through the various seasons of our life or when we experience life-quakes!

## A FLAVOUR-ful Life—A Hypothesis

Playing to full potential, I have come to learn, involves a delicate balancing act across six broad dimensions that are presented below. As you go through this, I would urge you not to look at this as a sequence or in a linear form but really see this as six dimensions that we need to concurrently straddle with deliberate intent and deal with the interplay across these.

The six dimensions are:

**F** – Discern and influence the **Family** context
**L** – Make space for what you **Love**
**A** – Tune into **Aspirations** and make consistent choices
**VO** – Strive to be of **Value** by seeking/creating **Opportunity**
**U** – Invest in yoUrself
**R** – Cultivate Healthy **Relationships**

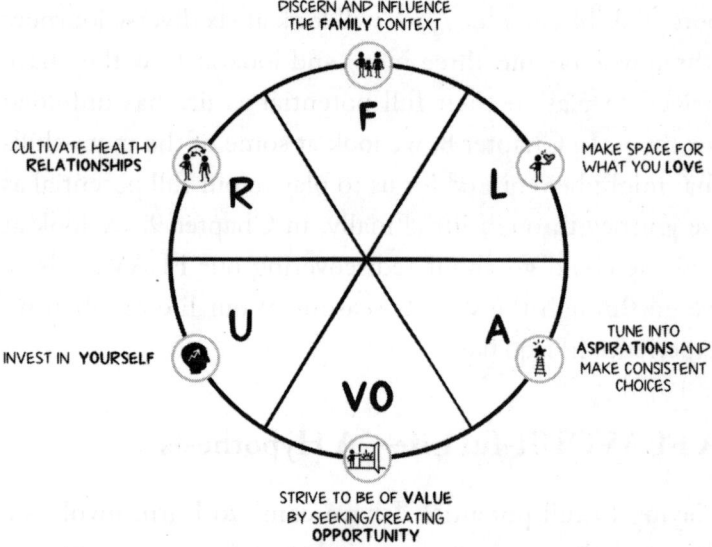

Let me lay out each of the elements in detail for your consideration. I should state at the outset that the sequence in which these are laid out does not have to be the sequence in which you process them in your life.

## F—Discern and influence the Family context

We do not solve the jigsaw of life in isolation. We do that in the context of a team and that team is the family. How we play a certain situation is often a function of the team situation. In the ICC Cricket World Cup final in Ahmedabad on 19 November 2023, Australia beat India to win its sixth title. Marnus Labuschagne scored 58 in 110 balls in the final. In most situations, that knock would be seen as a failure in this format. In this context, it helped them win the cup given that Travis Head made 137 in 120 balls. If you are the goalkeeper of a football team, then we would be wrong to measure your worth in terms of the number of goals you scored. The worth of homemakers who hold the fort (very often forsaking their own careers) cannot be measured in monetary terms. They often choose to play their role in the context of the family situation they are in. I notice that we all play a certain role given the situation we find ourselves in. What playing to full potential means is often determined by our unique family context. When I say family, in most situations given the current social fabric in India, it boils down to our spouse, our children, our parents and in some instances, our siblings. Very often this is the small group of people whose lives and fortunes are closely intertwined.

The first and foremost point to mention here is being aware that our personal operating system is shaped by the family context in which we grow up. It is important to recognize that as we take stock of our situation and our choices. While we all evolve and change over time, there is something about the foundational influences which stay with us for long. In some cases, this can also be about driving closure with the past or overcoming childhood trauma. Soma Biswas Vajpayee, an individual who is profiled as an exemplar of striving to play to full potential in the next chapter, speaks about how domestic violence during her childhood shaped her beliefs and choices. She stayed shackled to her past, till she proactively worked on coming to terms with it and getting closure. Only then, she says, she has been able to start playing to her full potential.

The second element of family worth tuning into is that of money. It is important to take stock of the money element, both in terms of the current wealth and monetary objectives for the future. Very often, I find people operating under false constraints of money when it stops being a crucial factor. In my previous role as a search consultant, I would often interact with candidates who have crossed the point of financial independence (by a factor of two or more) but still would make choices about the next career move based on which opportunity would pay them more. Aparna, whose father and grandfather run a successful metal alloy business in Tamil Nadu, kept telling herself for a long time that she wanted to be financially independent. That got her down the path of B.Com and CA and professional practice. When she interned at the company and spent time across various roles, she enjoyed the CSR stint the most. Much more than the commercial parts of the business that she had been trained for. After going through a period of dissonance, she came to the realization that rather than being stubborn about going after commercial roles, she could stay true to her context, be honest about her financial reality and do what gave her joy without being shackled by the false constraint of money. She signed up for an MSW course at TISS, Mumbai and now is really flourishing as a social worker. While I do believe that economic independence is a healthy goal to strive towards for men and women, the answer often is quite contextual. If the pursuit of economic outcomes is not joyful and/or comes in the way of other more important elements in life that need your time and attention—whether you are a man or a woman—it is worth asking the question if it is worth it! The harsh reality is that the effort required to earn a lakh varies from person to person and there is a time implication of money that needs to be looked at here as well.

The third element of family worth tuning into is the various transitions that are underway in the family—maternity, arrival of a child, children approaching classes 11 and 12 that require additional time and attention, empty nesting, retirement and so on. This often has implications on demands on our time and attention. Sometimes the transitions are gradual, sometimes sudden. In the case of dual-career couples, there might often be a timing mismatch between the role transitions (often including relocation) of the husband and wife. Whether we like it or not, family context plays a big role in how we shape our lives.

Finally, the family context in many situations determines the resources that are available for pursuing one's career. I know of many men and women who are able to pursue their professional ambitions because their parents or in-laws are next door to them and can take care of the children when they return from school during their formative years. In some cases, one has to assume responsibility for caregiving for ageing parents. Some of these elements can impact the residual bandwidth we have and the choices we make around career and intensity.

In addition, I have noticed that people who play to their full potential proactively influence their family context by negotiating with the key people around them. They don't treat the context around them as a given. Dr Stew Friedman[1] (🎤) has studied work-life integration for close to four decades, and he speaks about how we all have a responsibility to carry the key stakeholders along with us in our journey. This includes our colleagues at work and our family members. Our goals and plans are of no use if we are not able to get a buy-in from the people around us. Amish Tripathi[2] (🎤), a best-selling author, has spoken about the transition phase when he was a senior leader in the financial services sector, at the cusp of moving to writing. He speaks about how he enrolled his family in his decision towards writing, and how much difference it made to him to have their support as he walked that path.

Needless to say, each situation is bespoke, and each family context is unique. But I have noticed that people playing to their full potential handle this element with remarkable dexterity and tact. This requires a nuanced awareness of the family context across the various dimensions—financial circumstances, demands on time, transitions underway and irreversible windows that don't open again. It is the equivalent of reading the pitch before you decide on the game strategy. Ignore it at your own peril.

## L—Make space for what you Love

The one element I have come to learn in the context of playing to full potential is the role of 'play'. I have discovered that beyond a point it is rather hard for us to 'work' to our potential. Very often, 'play' is seen as something that children get involved in and not something for adults. We play when we do something we love and something that energizes us. In my empirical research, I have found that people who have some element of play in their lives show up better in the various facets of their lives. I feel there are three levels at which we could engage with what we love.

At the first level, we could align what we truly love with our 'work'. This is along the lines of what ikigai would suggest. The phrase 'work hard, play hard' becomes less relevant in that scenario. It just ends up feeling like a continuum of play. While there are many technical explanations to the word 'play', I would suggest a simple filter. Does the activity replenish you/energize you/ stimulate you? Or does it drain you/deflate you/dull you? There could be some elements of work that might be energizing and some not, but the key is to ensure that to the extent possible, we align the two. And this is a work in progress as we go through our journey. When I transitioned from McKinsey to Egon Zehnder, I moved from having conversations around strategy and business to discussing people and leadership. When I moved from Egon Zehnder to what I do now, I felt I had moved from having evaluative conversations with people as a search consultant to having enabling conversations as a coach or learning conversations as a podcaster which seems closer to what I truly love and find energizing. To that extent, work feels like play.

I feel each one of us has more agency than we think to get closer to what is play by either picking professions or pathways within professions which are in line with who we are and how we are wired. One of the people I coached was an associate principal in a prestigious consulting firm. He was distinctive at problem-solving and strategic thinking, but the people relationship element did not come naturally to him whether it was with the clients or internal team members. He kept getting poor scores in the upward feedback from his team and felt frustrated that he wasn't able to move the needle there despite his best intentions and make the promotion to partner. We went through our coaching sessions and discovered that there was an expert track in the organization that would be in line with how he was wired. He spends a lot more time 'playing' there today and is more fulfilled than earlier.

However, I recognize that many of us have commercial constraints within which we operate and 'playing' may not yield the commercial outcomes that we desire. Or often, we may not even know what 'play' is. It is a journey of discovery and evolution. The second level of engaging with something we love is making space for it as a serious pursuit somewhere in our lives.

Siddharth Gopalakrishnan is a partner at McKinsey leading the demanding life of a consultant. But he is actively involved in cricket and plays about twenty-five games every season across three teams including a team that includes dads from the school that his children go to. He states that he was in the Mumbai Under-16 probables but at that stage decided to prioritize studies over cricket. But he has now found a way to bring back his passion from his childhood and integrate that into his life. He has spoken about how his experiences on the cricket field energized him and made him a better leader in McKinsey.

Vivek Sunder is the CEO of Kerala Ayurveda Limited. After spending two decades in P&G, he worked as a COO at Swiggy and CEO at CueMath. He has also been pursuing wildlife photography since 2015. He credits photography for how it has improved his patience, focus, resilience and agility as a leader. 'I had to do three different safari trips over a year, and over 300 tries before I got the one keeper shot where everything was as expected and I got all my actions right,' he discusses, alluding to the resilience and perseverance that photography builds in a person.

Shashi Raghunandan is the CEO of Oaken, a B2B SaaS platform on a mission to expand farmland and resources. He has been painting with water colours for the last twenty-plus years. He is a keen student of painting and has sharpened his craft over the years. He speaks about how relaxing and therapeutic painting is as a pursuit. He also speaks about how it has made him a better observer of the world around him.

These people not only make the space for what they love but also reap the benefits of this pursuit in their careers as it makes them better in their jobs. Albert Einstein, it is said, flourished as a scientist because of his violin, not despite it!

I started learning to play the guitar in 2002 and continue to learn on Sundays. When I play songs with meaningful lyrics, the experience nourishes my soul and helps me bring my heart into what I do professionally. It has also helped me create memories with my wife who likes to sing, my son who is also learning to play the guitar, and my daughter who is learning to play the piano.

The third and possibly the most distant way of engaging with something we love is to find space for appreciating something that we truly love. Professional lives can be demanding, and one may not have the bandwidth to pursue what one loves in a hands-on way. You might not have time to play cricket, but do you make space for watching games? You may not have the capacity to play for a band but at least you make time to attend concerts and other performances. You get the drift. In Chapter 8, we will look at the four-way wins that talk about how we can be smart about pursuing some of these possibilities given the limited time we have at our disposal.

## A—Tune into Aspirations and make consistent choices

I have come to realize that a lot of us, especially in a country like India, are driven by our ambition which is often about what we want to become on the professional front. But life is much more than that. Instead of the word ambition, I find the word aspiration more holistic and empowering in the context of playing to full potential. People who are playing to their full potential, I notice, have aspirations for various facets of their lives. It might revolve around their hobbies, their children, their health, their relationships or any other element. Professional and commercial outcomes are often an element of the aspiration. But the key is to recognize the hierarchy and see this as a subset of your aspiration and not the other way around where your professional ambition is all-consuming and your other aspirations end up as a residual nice-to-have! The other element to bear in mind is to not fall victim to the default stereotypes for aspiration that might exist based on gender, parental backgrounds, the community we belong to, or other broad brushes people might use to categorize us. It is critical to embrace our individuality in the way we think about our unique aspirations across the various domains of life. You might also notice that ambition is often 'outside-in' while aspiration is 'inside-out' in the way it manifests. The transition from focusing on ambition to tuning into our aspiration is also about us moving our locus of control from the external world to our internal compass.

If somebody had asked me the question 'who are you?' about a decade or so ago, my response would have been anchored either around my educational background (engineer, MBA) or my profession (management consultant). Anecdotally, I can say with reasonable conviction that this response would be given by at least 80 per cent or more of the people in the thirty to sixty year band, if asked. However, we all recognize that we are much more than what we have studied and our professional title.

An easy place to start is to recognize the various identities we have for ourselves across our professional and personal domains. In my case, I would say, husband, father, son, brother, coach and podcaster to name a few. In addition to these identities, we all pursue a few activities and harbour a few interests. In my case, I spend some time engaging with the development sector through the organization—Social Venture Partners. I like to play occasional cricket in my community. It is interesting to note that some of the activities, if pursued consistently, might result in an identity. For instance, if I am committed to the social sector and spend significant time over the next years, I might develop (or be given) the identity of a philanthropist. For now, these are just activities in my life.

Just like a venture capitalist allocates her/his capital across various start-ups, each one of us has to allocate our time and attention across our various identities and activities in a thoughtful manner. In some cases, we might already have aspirations which just need to be bubbled up to the surface in an explicit manner. In other cases, we might have to do the work to articulate the aspiration clearly for each of the activities and identities. Unfortunately, this is not something that any of us is taught. Very often, we end up working with the expectations that society has of us without being intentional about it. We discuss the 'how' in some detail in Chapter 8.

To put it in simple terms, getting an A+ in one's career with a C or D in other subjects of life such as family, relationships, community service and hobbies does not make a good report card if we want to play to our full potential in the ongoing exam called life!

While aspiration is the third element I am listing in FLAVOUR, it often is the starting point as we think about our various macro and micro life choices along the journey.

## VO—Strive to be of Value by seeking/creating Opportunity

Dan Pink, in his widely famous TED talk around the Puzzle of Motivation,[3] speaks about three things required to motivate people—autonomy, mastery and purpose. The words are quite self-explanatory. We seek some agency in what we do (autonomy), we look for an element of excellence (mastery) and seek inspiration from the 'why' (purpose). While I agree with the pursuit of autonomy and mastery, I have found that the word 'purpose' can be daunting for many. As we discussed in the previous chapter, I empirically notice that it often emerges along the way and is not the starting point.

I feel that the people who play to their full potential just get started by looking at their skills, assets and capabilities and look for talent-market fit just like businesses seek product-market fit. The nature of what they end up doing is a function of their aspiration, family context and what they love—the themes we just discussed. They may not know their purpose on Day 1 but they discover that along the way as they walk the path by taking baby steps in a certain direction.

Many individuals have built and are building great institutions (for-profit businesses, social enterprises, non-profits) and all those are leaders who are striving to add value at scale and trying to make a dent by solving intractable problems facing the world. I have tremendous respect for these leaders who are making a significant difference in the world. For a long time, I felt I had to be like them. Dream big. Make a big dent. I have come to realize that given my aspirations to lead a harmonious life and make time for other pursuits, the pathway of an independent consultant would be the most appropriate (as of now) as it gives me the time and autonomy to pursue what I like. This life architecture, I believe, gives me greater joy than building a large organization that solves the same need. I draw my inspiration from the book *Small Giants: Companies That Choose to Be Great Instead of Big*. The book features several companies that have been deliberate about staying small because they believe that growth might dilute the secret sauce of the company. The reasons that make it exceptional and fun for the people in it. Somewhere, there is a default assumption in everyone's mind that we all need to think scale. I have come to realize that chasing scale may not be a joyful pursuit for everybody. It certainly is not for me. I realize that each one of us needs to find a way in which we can be of value given our capabilities, aspirations, family context and what we love. I think about impact in two broad frames:

*High touch, low reach:* this is the advisory work I do with a few leaders where I spend time with them and help them play to their unique and full potential.

*Low touch, high reach:* I create content that can provoke reflection and unlock potential.

Running an organization with a large team does not excite me. So, I have chosen an architecture that is lean, helps me stay artisanal and gives me the leeway to spend time on activities that energize me.

When I look at retired individuals who are leading a full life, there is an element of them being of value to the world around them. My father-in-law, Brigadier (Retired) V. Mahalingam is an Indian Army veteran. He fought in the Indo–Pakistan War of 1971 which resulted in the liberation of Bangladesh. When he retired, he went through a period of identity vacuum where he questioned his self-worth. Slowly he started pouring his energies into studying geopolitics, an area of passion. Today, he writes for several military publications and appears in the mainstream media on related topics. It gives him meaning and, more importantly, it provides him with self-worth.

He has found a way of being of value and the opportunity to be of value has evolved over the years as he has walked the path.

While this construct (of being of value and seeking opportunity) is relevant in the context of people pursuing active careers trying to stay relevant and trying to lead a full life, I feel it applies as much to homemakers (who are often women who give up a career post maternity to focus on the family), a large section of the population. When I look at homemakers who are happy, fulfilled and thriving, I notice that there is an element of being of value to people beyond the immediate family. While I do not downplay the role of a homemaker and what he/she does at home, I notice that the home is often a low feedback and a low gratitude environment. In addition, contributions towards children often pay off in the long run. By the time the tree takes shape, people often forget to acknowledge the gardener who planted the seed and watered the sapling in its early years. I also notice that there is a very close interplay between being of value to others and self-worth. When people commit to the family at the exclusion of everything else, their self-worth often starts eroding over time. I have noticed that even a small initiative to be of value outside the family can have a disproportional impact on self-worth and can set off a chain reaction that can lead to great outcomes.

My sister Nandhini and brother-in-law Muralikrishnan (Murali) live in Bengaluru. Murali is the president of Xiaomi India and Nandhini has chosen to play the role of the homemaker in the family. Nandhini has always been passionate about the arts from her childhood and used to excel in making Tanjore paintings, a traditional Indian art form characterized by rich and vivid colours and glittering gold foils overlaid on delicate but extensive gesso work with an inlay of glass beads and pieces of semi-precious gems. Given the financial context in her house, she decided to focus on being a homemaker. However, along the way, she happened to be diagnosed with multiple sclerosis, an autoimmune condition. A combination of these factors led her to go through a phase of frustration and an identity vacuum. Of late, she has developed an interest in mandala art, a geometric art form. She has an Instagram account[4] and showcases her work to others and it has given her a sense of happiness and fulfilment as she strives to bring her skills to add value to others by giving them products that they love. My mother, Brindha Jayaraman, has been a homemaker all through her life. I am grateful for her sacrifices in bringing me and my sister up. When my father passed away in 2008, there was a big vacuum in her life. However, she learnt the methods of acupuncture and acupressure and would treat people as a way of giving back. Even if she met one patient a week, it brought her a lot of meaning and that impacted the way she showed up in her other interactions. Recently, one of her close friends lost her husband and my mother has been a comforting shoulder, helping her grapple with life post the loss, given she went through a similar phase herself fifteen years ago. I have observed that these small initiatives outside the close circle of family can do wonders to self-worth which in turn can spur people to do bigger and better things over time.

I have come to believe that whether one is an entrepreneur building a unicorn, a retiree, a philanthropist, a social worker or a homemaker, it is critical that we strive to be of value to others beyond the immediate family. When we do this in line with our talent, passions, family context and our aspirations, it does wonders to our self-worth and puts on the path of playing to our full potential. This does require us to be entrepreneurial, engage in the talent-market dating process by experimenting and strive to make a difference, irrespective of the shape of what we embark on.

## U—Invest in yoUrself

We are living in a world where given advances in healthcare, we are likely to live longer lives. There is a reasonable chance that we will live into our nineties and beyond. The sheer economics of this might mean that we might have to strive to be of value and keep seeking opportunities (as discussed earlier) well into our seventies for us to sustain this lifespan. For us to stay relevant with the changing seasons of our lives, I believe we need to think about investing in ourselves on three fronts.

- Self-awareness
- Physical, mental and spiritual health
- Skills and capabilities

*Self-awareness*

As you would have gleaned by now, if we want to play to our unique and full potential, a non-negotiable prerequisite is our self-awareness (how we see ourselves, how others see us and what truly matters to us). Chapters 3, 4 and 5 are about getting in touch with ourselves. I cannot emphasize this any further.

*Physical, mental and spiritual health*

If I told you that the Indian cricket team batting first has a score of 150 runs for 6 wickets in 15 overs and then asked you if this is a good score, what would you say? The answer is that it depends on the context. Of course, it depends on the opposition's bowling attack and the pitch and the weather conditions etc. But a crucial question would be to understand the format that is being played. Is it a T20, 50 overs or a Test match? If it is a T20 match, a score of 150 runs for the loss of six wickets by the time 3/4th of the innings has ended is a healthy place to be and one could imagine a good finish. However, if it is a 50-over game, 15 overs are just 30 per cent of the innings and losing 6 wickets is worrisome. If we take a 100-year life as a reference point, I see several people (I include my younger self in this list) who are huffing and puffing around the 30 per cent mark. We might have runs on the board but we might have lost just too many wickets in life! This segment is about shining the light on our 'personal balance sheet', our health.

There is a point to be made about the correlation between the intensity of our work and our health. We have finite hours in the day and it does not take a rocket scientist to discern the link between the time and energy we spend at work and the time we spend on our health. I remember a recent conversation with the CEO of a large listed company. When I asked him what his weekend looks like, he said, 'Recovery!'

We need to take care of our bodies and focus on our physical fitness. However, we mustn't get obsessive about it. Tom Vanderbilt[5] (🎤) speaks about how he ended up being a part of a cycling group in New York and suddenly got drawn into the competitive spirit which beyond a point becomes counterproductive. He says that there is a group of middle-aged men in New York who pursue interests like running, cycling and swimming with a certain misplaced sense of obsession. He quips that there is a term used to describe this archetype—MAMIL (Middle-Aged Men in Lycra). The group of people that gear up with all kinds of fancy equipment and set ambitious goals for themselves and push themselves beyond their limits. I went through a similar experience when I started running long distances. I trained for my first half marathon with a group called Striders and clocked 2:09:00 in 2013. Trying to bring it down below two hours was a goal at that time that consumed me. There was a certain musicality to a sub-2-hour half marathon. I managed to do that the following year, in 2014. Then 1:45:00 became the next goalpost. Shaving every minute of my time was also getting exponentially harder as time went by, increasing my frustration with it. Till my wife asked me one day, 'Why is this important?' I realized that I was turning into a MAMIL with a misplaced sense of drive and ambition which was impacting other domains of my life. I notice that type A people who like to push themselves at work, without realizing it, end up taking a similar approach to health which sometimes can be counterproductive. It is worth asking, if the pursuit is 'fit for purpose' in the context of my life.

Similarly, we need to be aware of our mental health situation and proactively seek help if required. It hit me hard personally when we recently lost a senior banker in the financial services world who lived in my gated community to issues around mental health. He was in his mid-forties and has two children (aged nine and seven) and one of them is friends with my son. He decided to jump and end his life leaving his wife and children behind. This might be an extreme case, but I guess people are dealing with mental health challenges along a spectrum of severity. If we find ourselves in a situation where we need external help such as counselling or therapy, we should consider being open about this. Fortunately, getting help is becoming less of a taboo, and more people are recognizing the value of taking care of their mental health

Spiritual health is a relatively new domain for me. I have come to realize that spiritual health is a subjective and personal concept, and different individuals may define it in various ways based on their beliefs and experiences. For some, it may involve religious practices, while for others, it may be more about finding purpose and connection in non-religious ways. I have had friends that tell me about Vipassana, some speak about spending time poring over the Bhagwad Gita. Currently, I find spirituality in some of the philanthropic work I do with the group Social Venture Partners[6]. It gives me meaning and gratitude and reminds me of my insignificance in the grand scheme of things. Each one of us needs to find an activity beyond us and our close circle where we engage, learn and develop some perspective around our place in the world.

## Invest in skills and capabilities

We used to live in a time when people led a life with three discrete stages—study, work and retire. Lynda Gratton[7] says that earlier when we knew people's age, we knew their stage. Now the two seem decoupled. Staying relevant is a life-long journey and we must keep sharpening our axe as we go through our journey. It could be a combination of going deeper in the area that we are good at and investing in adjacencies that could open up possibilities. Lynda Gratton goes on to say that we could think of ourselves as the Greek symbol 'π'. She mentions that if we pay close attention to the symbol, one is a straight leg and the other has a curve in the end. She says the straight leg is about going deep and planting roots in one space that gives us expertise in an area. The bent leg is about developing capabilities in adjacent spaces and the top horizontal line of the symbol is about integrating these capabilities and bringing them to bear to be of value.

In my case, after I left Egon Zehnder to pursue the journey of coaching in 2016, initially it was about developing certification and capabilities as a coach. Subsequently, it turned into being curious and learning about podcasting. The last few months have been about developing the skill of writing long-form coherently.

Skills and capabilities are not just about sharpening the saw in the professional space. Sometimes, they could just be about learning a pursuit that gives you joy. There may not be any visible ROI at that time. When I was living in Chennai in 2003, I remember KPMG, the firm I worked with at that time, decided to participate in a corporate regatta organized by the Madras Boat Club. Some of us got trained in rowing for a few months and then participated in it. When it concluded, they gave away awards for the oarsmen and oarswomen who finished on the podium. I was not good enough for any of that. They also had a separate award for the most improved oarsman, and I was chosen for it. That has stayed with me ever since. This experience taught me to bring a beginner's mindset and focus on the slope of the curve rather than where I am. I do not think I could have anticipated learning this lesson when I signed up for the regatta.

I have found that a lot of us, by default, end up investing in things that feed our heads. I have noticed that investing in things that nourish our hearts as well to be of great value.

It could be painting, cooking, gardening, wine tasting or anything else. Anything that gets us to feel, not just think.

As we think about playing to potential over the long game, it becomes that much more important for us to manage our personal balance sheet—tangible and intangible, head, hand and heart—as we walk the path.

## R—Cultivate healthy Relationships

Relationships are a key element of intangible assets that is worth shining light on. An eighty-year study of happiness at Harvard Medical School by Dr Robert Waldinger[8] has shown that close relationships and social connections are the #1 factor responsible for our well-being as we age. Prof. Herminia Ibarra[9] (🎙) speaks about three types of networks that are crucial for us—personal networks (like the one that Dr Waldinger's study alludes to) that help us stay happy and alive, operational networks (ones that help us get the job done today) and strategic networks (the connections that help us access new ecosystems and possibilities).

I find that there are some relationships that one needs to cultivate that could yield returns over the long term. When I was a search consultant at Egon Zehnder, I could see the difference between candidates who would strategically invest the time to build relationships with search consultants (in a constructive way) rather than those who reached out when they needed a job. Some individuals would go out of the way to make connections and suggest other candidates that could be relevant for the search and share industry insights that would help me get better. One of the entrepreneurs I worked with, Rajesh Singh,[10] regularly gets his team to recommend one colleague from their previous organization that he could potentially recruit. He then asks his assistant to reach out to those potential candidates and has 'no agenda' conversations when there is no hiring need for him. He also finds a way of keeping in touch occasionally through greetings and wishes. But when these individuals go through a lean patch in their job, they often reach out to him, and he laps them up at often below-market rates. Whatever our field, there is an opportunity to look beyond the here and now and build some of these strategic relationships proactively.

I also notice that those who play to their full potential seem to find a way of having meaningful relationships with various groups beyond the family (friends from high school, undergrad, post-grad, work, fellow hobbyists, neighbours, parents of kids' friends). I love one of the old Airtel advertisements which went, '*Har ek friend zaroori hota hai* [Every friend is important].' Each of these cohorts seems to bring a certain diversity of thought and emotion that can enrich the journey. It is critical to discuss what we mean by key relationships. We are not referring to 'deal friends'[11] but to 'real friends' where there is no agenda involved.

## Bringing FLAVOUR to Life

As we think about applying this approach to playing to full potential, I feel it is critical to underscore what it is not. It is clearly not a substitute to Ikigai. I do think there is a place for having a true north in our life. FLAVOUR is meant to be an attempt at providing us with a language to work with the messiness of life as we go through different phases. Going back to the quote from Lincoln in the previous chapter, FLAVOUR can hopefully help you navigate the swamps, chasms and deserts that you encounter as you walk towards your true north.

Here are some thoughts on how you can engage with it.

***Strive for coherence:*** As you would appreciate, FLAVOUR is not something that needs to be approached linearly one after the other, from F to R. We could start anywhere in the circle and move around the rest of it. The keyword to bear in mind is coherence. We often speak about the coherence of a business strategy. The various choices we make to run a business need to come together and ought to be consistent. The same, I believe, applies to finding our FLAVOUR. To that extent, all the elements are interconnected and not discrete and independent.

Reflecting on three questions can tell us if our approach to finding our FLAVOUR is coherent.

- Are we making key choices along F, L, VO, U and R in service of our Aspiration (A) which encompasses various dimensions of our life?;
- are we allocating adequate time and attention to the short-term (F, L, VO) and the long-term (U, R) without swinging too far one way or another?; and

- do we have a clear prioritization mechanism as we make micro trade-offs during the rough and tumble of daily life? Is there a consistent, well-articulated 'why' in our head when we choose to say yes or no to things that pull us too far in a certain dimension?

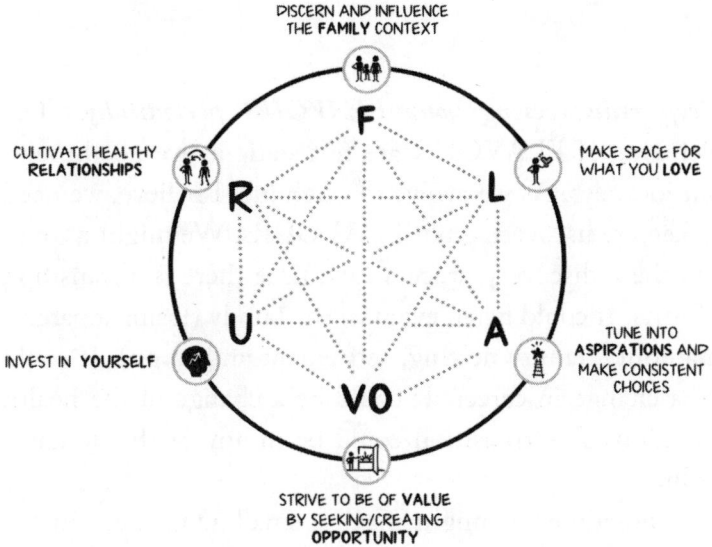

*May not have it all:* One could argue that if one has to play to full potential, then that would happen when we are 'hitting it out of the park' on all fronts. I have noticed that it is often hard to have it all! Every FLAVOUR we choose has some consequences and trade-offs. Two people are likely to assign different weights and emphasis on different elements of FLAVOUR that work for them.

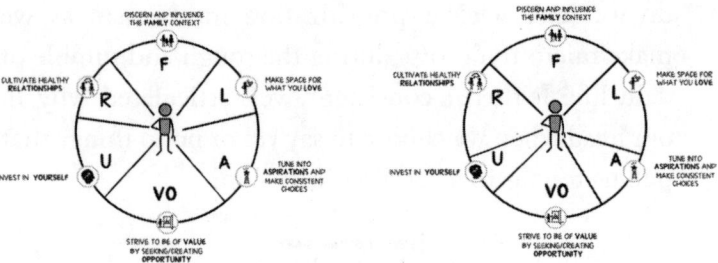

***Keep rediscovering your FLAVOUR periodically:*** The elements of FLAVOUR are not static as we go through our journeys. As we evolve through life, I believe, we need to keep rediscovering our FLAVOURs. We might have to run the rediscovery process each time there is a transition of sorts. It could be an event in the family (losing a parent, maternity, empty nesting, retirement and so on). It could be a change in career. It could be a change in the health situation. The transition could be in any of the domains of life.

Sometimes, it might mean a small adjustment in the various elements. Sometimes, we might have to pull the whole thing apart before we put it together. We might have to assess our approach based on what the transition measures on the Richter scale when it comes to the impact on our lives!

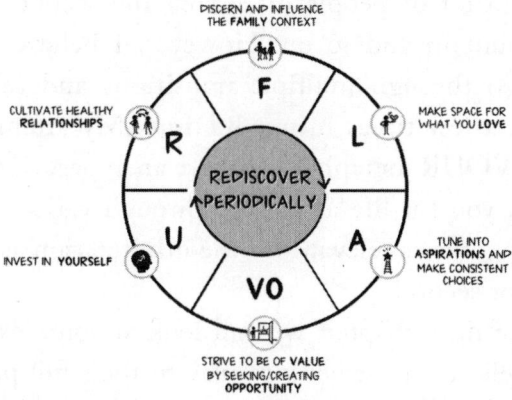

Ayse Birsel[12] (🎤), an industrial designer, who applies these principles to life design, speaks about how we can deconstruct our life and reconstruct it differently while staying true to what matters to us. She says that we could have the same base ingredients but end up with a different flavour depending on the recipe we use. She calls the process deconstruction-reconstruction. She asks us to strip down our current life into various sub-components such as health, work, friends and family, hobbies etc. and then asks us to be creative in how we reassemble some of these components based on our values, and what inspires us and the realities of our life.

The key is for us to recognize that this wheel needs to keep spinning as we go through life, especially during transitions (that we choose to embrace or the ones that are thrown at us). We could even envision this FLAVOUR wheel as a kaleidoscope whose pattern keeps evolving as we keep spinning the wheel over time and keep rediscovering our FLAVOUR periodically.

I see a lot of people discussing the second act, the third mountain and so on. However, I believe that we all will go through multiple transitions and reimagine ourselves a few times in our lifetime. My attempt with the FLAVOUR metaphor is to give an approach that will stay with you for life as you go through various phases. Hopefully, it is as relevant for the nth iteration as it is for the first or second.

In the next chapter, we will look at some exemplars who, I believe, are striving to play to their full potential. Using the FLAVOUR approach, we look at how they have straddled the various domains of life and rediscovered their FLAVOUR as the seasons have changed.

## Chapter Synthesis

Playing to full potential involves leading an intentional multi-dimensional life. This involves juggling the dimensions below (listed in no particular order).

### F—Discern and influence the Family context

For several people, it comes down to their spouse, children and parents. Four things are critical in this context: a) How our operating system is moulded by our family context as we grow up; b) financial context which is a function of the wealth/income that is available to us through our immediate family; and c) silent transitions that are often underway in the family that could have a bearing on the choices we make; and d) resources and support that is available from the family.

The key is to come to terms with the context but not treat it as a hard constraint. Smart people can influence the key family stakeholders around them to get to a meaningful outcome.

## L—Make space for what you Love

All of us must discern what feels like 'play' as we cannot work to our potential. We could only play to our potential! Tune into what energizes you and gets you into 'flow'; try to find it in your work (ideally), or else pursue a hobby that energizes you or build space for appreciating something that you love (and that preferably engages your heart).

## A—tune into your Aspiration (not just ambition)

We all play various roles in our lives and a healthy aspiration often is multi-dimensional which accounts for the different identities that we carry with us as we go through our journey.

## VO—Strive to be of Value by seeking/creating Opportunity

Just like we speak about product–market fit, we all need to be deliberate about talent–market fit. We need to take stock of our capabilities, networks, our passions and go on a dating process to discover where we can be of value. A pre-requisite for that is working on our self-worth.

## U—Invest in yoUrself

We must invest in our self-awareness and in our physical, mental and spiritual health and capabilities to be able to play the long game.

## R—Cultivate healthy Relationships

Enough research suggests that healthy relationships are key to a full and fulfilling life. We must invest in personal relationships outside of family and transformative relationships in the professional space.

FLAVOUR doesn't have to be approached linearly. It is circular. The key is to strive for coherence in our choices across the various dimensions and manage the tension therein. As we go through the key seasons of life, it is also critical to keep rediscovering our FLAVOUR and make trade-offs and choices aligned with the emerging context.

## Contextual Audio Snippets from the Podcast

- **Audio Clip 6.1:** Prof. Stew Friedman on work–life integration
- **Audio Clip 6.2:** Amish Tripathi on enrolling the people around us in our journey
- **Audio Clip 6.3:** Tom Vanderbilt on misplaced pursuit of mastery
- **Audio Clip 6.4:** Herminia Ibarra on three types of networks we should strive to cultivate
- **Audio Clip 6.5:** Ayse Birsel on deconstructing and reconstructing our life

# 7

# Some FLAVOUR-ful Lives

*Kya yeh ujaale*
*Kya yeh andhere*
*Donon se aage hai manzar tere*
*Kyon roshni tu baahar talashe*
*Teri mashaalein andar tere*

Why do you care about the light around when your
sights are far ahead
Why do you look for direction from the outside when
the fire burns so brightly within
> —Lyrics: Manoj Muntashir; song: 'Besabriyaan';
> movie: *MS Dhoni: The Untold Story*

During the summer of 2018, my family and I visited LEGO
House in Billund, Denmark—the birthplace of Lego. My
son had been playing with Lego for the last several years

and we were keen to see where it all started. I was also curious about visiting the birthplace of LEGO because the company truly believes in the role of play in unlocking human potential. I was as curious and excited as my son was when we visited the place.

LEGO House is a multi-storeyed building and in its 12,000 m$^2$ space, it is filled with twenty-five million LEGO bricks, LEGO waterfalls and giant animals and plants—all made of LEGO bricks. The house offers experiences for children and adults of all ages who want to develop creatively and explore the endless possibilities for learning through play. If you are a fan of Lego, then this is like a dream come true.

For several hours, we played and built various things in a world without any constraints of LEGO brick supply! But it was when we were leaving, that something fascinating happened. As a souvenir, they give each person a pack containing six red LEGO bricks (2x4). They also give you a design that is unique to you. Turns out, the six bricks can be spatially arranged in more than 900 million ways (915,103,765 ways to be precise).[1] They give you a design with which you can assemble the six bricks and say that the design cannot be replicated elsewhere in the world. To me, this intuitively captures the uniqueness of our lives across various dimensions.

The rest of this chapter profiles six individuals (three women and three men) who, I believe, are striving to play to their full potential in their own unique way. This is not to say that they are acing every dimension of FLAVOUR.

Clearly, there is tension involved in pursing the various elements. For instance, if you go all out on the professional front (VO), it could impact the time you have for what you love or investing in yourself. If you are guided by what you are passionate about (L), there is a chance that there are financial constraints and that can put pressure on the family front and the choices you can make. There is one thing that I have personally observed in the case of these individuals. There is a spring in their step, conviction in their choices and a resonance between what they are doing and who they are being as they walk their path. As I lay out some of these stories, do look out for the work they are doing around their self-awareness and tuning into their values. You can also glean how they manage the tension and strive for coherence and how they rediscover their FLAVOUR as their context evolves slowly or shifts dramatically. For the purposes of illustration, we have looked at each of the journeys along the six dimensions below that we laid out in the previous chapter.

**F** – Discern and influence the **Family** context
**L** – Make space for what you **Love**
**A** – Tune into **Aspirations** and make consistent choices
**VO** – Strive to be of **Value** by seeking/creating **Opportunity**
**U** – Invest in yoUrself
**R** – Cultivate healthy **Relationships**

In choosing the six, I have tried to bring in as much diversity as possible across dimensions. Hopefully, you will be able to relate to some of the elements of the journeys of these six inspiring individuals.

**Ravishankar Iyer's** journey resembles that of many of us who came from the middle class. We were told to hunker down and ace a few exams and that we would be set for life. We walk that path only to realize that it does not give us joy beyond a point. Then what does one do? The way he has taken risks and found his sweet spot in storytelling is inspiring.

**Sangeeta Shahaney** is a great exemplar of somebody who has managed to find different FLAVOURs for various phases of her life. Almost like in Test cricket, how teams play it session by session! I personally find her pivot from being a homemaker to an entrepreneur when she lost her husband, inspiring.

**Soma Biswas's** is a case of an individual coming to terms with some of her beliefs that she had held on to tightly since childhood and then choosing to go beyond that to find a playground that uniquely combined her passion for painting and her desire to do purposeful work. What is specifically remarkable is the way she has chosen to thrive despite the multiple changes in location across countries driven by her husband's career.

**Sucharita Mukherjee's** journey is an inspiring story of an individual rebounding from a personal crisis to shapeshift from an early career in investment banking in London to becoming a FinTech entrepreneur in Chennai driving financial inclusion. All this while raising two daughters.

**Sumeet Mehta**'s is a story of having the courage to hit the pause button in life, conducting a few experiments, listening to his heart and committing to a journey towards improving educational outcomes of millions of kids in small towns in India while building a purpose-led organization that is valued over USD 1 Billion.

**Vineet Panchhi** starts as a wannabe rock musician, ends up joining hotel management and then pursues multiple corporate jobs till he gets back to his hometown, Dehradun. That sets into motion a chain of events where he straddles multiple identities of poet, voice artist, filmmaker, singer, inspirational speaker and much more.

Each of the journeys (■◀[2]) presented here is layered and complex. There is no 'bumper sticker' wisdom to be shared here. I would urge you to specifically focus on:

- Their approach to building awareness about themselves—who they are and what mattered to them;
- the balance of head and heart as they made choices in their lives;
- a sense of agency they had even when their chips were down;
- their journey to rediscovering their FLAVOUR when they were at a point of inflection; and

- The fact that they 'don't have it all'; tune into how they handle the tension in FLAVOUR when it stretches them in different directions.

## Ravishankar Iyer (Ravi)—Discovering His FLAVOUR as a Storytelling Coach by Leaning into What He Loves

Ravi spent his formative years in Sion, Mumbai and Aurangabad, Maharashtra in a nurturing Indian middle-class family that valued the pursuit of Saraswati (Goddess of Learning) much more than Lakshmi (Goddess of Wealth).

Ravi started his career pretty traditionally, becoming a chartered accountant (national rank 11), and then getting an MBA from IIM Ahmedabad.

Ravi's journey from a rank-holding CA, to finally that of a storytelling coach is inspiring because his journey is led by tuning into what he loves. He has architected a successful lifestyle business that lets him pursue his love for storytelling while earning adequately and allowing him time for non-work pursuits.

Ravi currently lives in Pune, with his wife Praveena, who runs Amazeum: an experiential learning centre for kids—and his two kids, aged twelve and six. Let us look at some of the elements of FLAVOUR in the context of Ravi's journey.

**A—Tune into Aspiration and make consistent choices**

Over the years, Ravi's aspiration has been largely around leading an 'inside-out' life by tuning into what brings him joy. 'Somewhere in my teens or early twenties, I realized that blindly chasing higher pay packages was a fool's errand because I would see folks who were earning much more than me comparing themselves with people earning more than them and complaining about not having enough!' he says.

Today, Ravi aspires to continue the pursuit of mastery in his craft of storytelling at work. He also aims to explore adjacent areas such as the use of storytelling in education, science, history and society. In doing so, he aspires to achieve a balance between the financial outcomes, fun and fulfilment he gets from work and the time and effort he puts into it. He also proactively ensures that he gets enough family time along the way.

**L—Make space for what you Love**

Ravi's love for reading—and hence storytelling—began when he first visited a lending library with his father, in Class two. From his very first book, a Chacha Choudhary comic, he was hooked! His love for reading has seen him traverse through the worlds of Tinkle, Amar Chitra Katha, Enid Blyton and Robert Ludlum, to non-fiction, which he now almost exclusively reads.

Professionally, he discovered storytelling, when one of his management consulting clients told him to 'not just dump data but tell a story while making a presentation'.

This was also around the time he read the book *Made to Stick* by Chip and Dan Heath. That started him on a path of leading with a narrative in his presentations. Over the years, he discovered that he loved making complex ideas simple and teaching them—and saw that he had been doing that even in situations he did not need to such as while taking tuition sessions for his MBA batchmates, training new hires at Feedback Infra, the management consulting job he worked at after IIMA.

Storytelling offers a unique blend of structure and creativity, something that resonates deeply with Ravi. He credits his love for structure to his father who was extremely organized and disciplined, and his love for creativity to his mother, somebody who wrote poetry, conducted music classes, and was creatively inclined.

## VO—Strive to be of Value by seeking/creating Opportunity

Ravi's journey to discovering storytelling as his 'sweet spot' is a non-linear one, driven by his curiosity and passion.

After his CA, he worked at L&T as an executive assistant to the CFO. In this stint, he realized that while he had excelled in finance as a student, it did not excite him as a professional. Post IIMA, he joined as a management consultant at Feedback Infra, where he worked for seven years. He quit to join B-ABLE, a start-up working to solve the employability problem in India. In his three years there, he realized that the model had market challenges.

Around that time, a trip to some South Indian temples reignited his passion for history, and he co-founded the start-up CaptivaTour that would tell audio stories about historic monuments in India through a mobile app. CaptivaTour struggled to monetize its content, and when his income dipped to approximately 15 per cent of his consulting income, Ravi decided to try his hand at training workshops with an organization doing the same: Mind Matters.

Conducting a couple of workshops for Mind Matters led him, very quickly, to what would become his niche—conducting workshops that focused on storytelling with data.

The initial years of this journey, which he started in mid-2016, were quite tough, Ravi admits. But over the years, he has built a robust business with a strong client base that includes top firms in India.

Ravi also strives to be of value by offering his skills at deeply discounted fees and sometimes pro bono to organizations that might need it; for instance, he has worked with Social Venture Partners, a non-profit, to help their mentee organizations with storytelling.

## U—Invest in yoUrself

Ravi has clearly invested in his self-awareness, tuning into what gives him joy and what feels like play. He has also been deliberate about his unique skill-stack (finance background, consulting skills, data interpretation, weaving stories, passion for writing and teaching) and brings it to bear in various things he does.

Over the years, Ravi has focused on learning and growing within the discipline so that he can sharpen his craft. He spends 40-50 per cent of his time on research and creation, the part of work he calls 'fun'. He reads extensively, listens to podcasts, writes regularly through his newsletter, social media and website and attends workshops by others to learn from them. The *Story Rules* podcast that he curates is an exercise in learning and growing within his space.

## F—Discern and influence Family context

'I told Praveena before we got married that I might leave my job one day to join a not-for-profit or to do something on my own,' he says. Having his wife's support has been crucial in enabling Ravi to find what he loves to do, especially when the going got hard. He also admits that, while they have not had to dip into the safety net, they do have one. 'Praveena's father is an incredibly successful entrepreneur,' he said.

While Ravi is candid that 'work is my first love', his flexible work schedule allows him ample time to balance home and family. He works for about twenty days every month, which leaves him enough time to pursue his hobbies and spend time with his family and friends. 'I have a lot of time,' he said.

## R—Cultivate healthy Relationships

Ravi confesses that he is a private individual with a small but close social network, and prefers deep conversations with a small set of close friends.

Overall Ravi considers his journey to still be an ongoing one. Even about the 'successful' parts of the journey (say the last three to four years), he said, 'I have wrestled with self-doubt and imposter syndrome. But I've found that actions like speaking to my wife, friends like you, and specifically, a coach I have worked with in Pune, have been immensely useful in managing these difficult periods.'

\* \* \*

Ravi and his wife Praveena are exemplars of an authentic and contended life where they have reflected deeply on what gives them joy and they are living it out in a way that gives them time to smell the roses on their journey.

## Sangeeta Shahaney—Adapting to Life's Various Seasons with Different FLAVOURs

Sangeeta is a sought-after SAT[3] coach based in Pune. She was born to upper-middle-class Sindhi parents in South

Mumbai—where she also spent her formative years—who had both come to India as refugees during the partition and rebuilt their lives through a strong work ethic.

A graduate in human resources from the prestigious Tata Institute of Social Sciences, Sangeeta's foray into entrepreneurship came rather late: in her mid-forties as a response to losing her husband to cancer.

With her innate work ethic and entrepreneurial skills, she has built a successful lifestyle business that now, fourteen years after she started it, runs pretty much on autopilot.

Sangeeta has two loving, grown-up children and is a doting grandmother to her one-year-old granddaughter.

Her's is a case of playing to potential by keeping things simple, looking at reality in the eye and taking one pragmatic baby step at a time to strive to lead a FLAVOUR-ful life.

Let us look at some of the elements of FLAVOUR in the context of Sangeeta's journey.


**F—Discern and influence Family context**

'Family first' is the lens that has influenced Sangeeta's choices and the shape of her journey.

She was deeply influenced by her dad's work ethic. However, it was her mother's nurturing instinct that she has really absorbed and embodied throughout her life.

'Being able to shape how another human being turns out is such a privilege,' she said.

Sangeeta spent her early career years helping her father, one of the pioneers of executive search in India, set up his business.

Despite having the option of continuing to work with her dad full-time, she chose to marry for love and travelled the world with her Merchant Navy husband. During those years, she worked part-time for her father. 'I used to be researching and posting documents to him from different ports,' she recollected.

Once her kids were born, she took a break to focus on the family. When they were a little older, she began using her free time to volunteer at Akanksha Foundation, a non-profit.

She chose volunteering as she could be home before her younger child returned from school. But her innate work ethic meant that she treated volunteering as a serious commitment. She showed up on fixed days and at fixed times, for five years. 'I had my own business card. I was part of important initiatives at Akanksha,' she says with pride.

In the summer of 2009, her husband was diagnosed with cancer and passed away shortly after. While they were comfortable financially, her kids were young. 'I have always been a planner,' she says. 'I wanted to plan for unknown future expenses and supplement our nest egg.' This, combined with her fluency and love for English is what led her towards SAT coaching.

## VO—Strive to be of Value by seeking/creating Opportunity

Once she decided to get into SAT coaching in 2010, Sangeeta spent six months working with a local institute to understand what SAT coaching was about. There she discovered the market opportunity: there was a need, but nobody was really doing a good job of it in Pune.

That got her to jump into the deep end, with a close friend who was her business partner. They started small: they had only two students coming to them in the beginning. However, Sangeeta's keen business mind meant she was always looking to grow the business. In a couple of years, they were running multiple batches to cater to the various dates for the SAT exam. After her partner moved to another country, instead of shutting shop, Sangeeta doubled down and decided to grow the business further. She opened another centre in Pune to cut students' commute times. In 2016, she partnered with a math tutor to offer comprehensive SAT coaching for both English and math under her roof. During the pandemic, Sangeeta moved her classes online. This has resulted in her catering to a small but growing number of students both pan India and worldwide.

However, with constant conversations around scrapping the SAT, and many colleges making the SAT optional for admissions, Sangeeta has consciously chosen to maintain the status quo instead of scaling the business any further.

## A—Tune into Aspiration and make consistent choices

Sangeeta frames her aspiration as being responsible in the various roles she plays—daughter, wife, mother, teacher and volunteer—and giving importance to the appropriate roles in the various seasons of her life.

'I have always seen life as it is, not as I think it should be,' she said. This has allowed her to respond to any situation with awareness, cheerfulness and resilience. Her aspiration has also evolved across life stages.

At her current life stage, when she is finally free of family responsibility, she says her aspirations are 'selfish' i.e. with her at the centre.

## L—Make space for what you Love

Sangeeta has always balanced her multiple priorities: caring for loved ones, pursuing her hobbies and taking care of her health, even when she was actively growing her business.

'There are three to four things I want to do,' she said, when she thinks about the decade ahead.

She has divided her priorities into giving back, mental agility, travelling and music.

She has joined the trusteeship of a school as a form of giving back. To stay mentally agile, she has actively sought out a mahjong community[4] and plays with them actively a few times a week. She travels often and is looking to join a choir to further her life-long love for music.

## R—Cultivate healthy Relationships

Sangeeta is a relationship-builder who has built and maintained close ties with extended family: cousins, in-laws, her daughters-in-law and some very close friends. Her relationships have been her support system and helped her overcome the loss of her husband. Today she also has deep friendships in her mahjong community.

## U—Investing in yoUrself

Sangeeta keeps life simple and has been self-aware about what was important to her at various stages of her life. She credits her secure childhood as something that has helped her to intuitively 'know' what was important when and prioritize accordingly.

\* \* \*

ENTREPRENEUR go with the flow TRAVELER

MAHJONG PLAYER

SANGEETA SHAHANEY

LOVES MUSIC, MAHJONG AND TRAVEL

TRAVEL SHAPED HER PERSPECTIVE

MAHJONG KEEPS MIND ACTIVE AND SHARP

ADAPTIVE in the way she adds value to the world

DAUGHTER MOTHER
VOLUNTEER TEACHER

ASPIRES TO BE RESPONSIBLE IN VARIOUS ROLES SHE PLAYS

Sangeeta's story is one of contentment and joy emerging from enjoying different FLAVOURs in different life seasons. She has tuned in to her gut and gone with the flow of life to strive to play to her full potential.

## Soma Biswas Vajpayee—Juggling Multiple Balls and Continually Reinventing Herself Across transitions

Soma is an artist and a practicing licensed art therapist based in New York, US. She lives with her husband Bhavtosh, a leading equity research analyst and investor, and their three children—two sons aged nineteen and seventeen and a daughter aged thirteen.

Soma grew up in the Steel Authority of India Limited township of Durgapur, West Bengal to a gynaecologist father and a homemaker mother. A bachelor of commerce and an MBA from IIM Ahmedabad, Soma started her career as a banker with Citibank. Her journey to becoming an art therapist traversed through several reinventions: coach, entrepreneur, artist and art therapist, each playing a role in expanding her self-awareness.

Along the way, she also learnt to embrace life's potential across its multiple dimensions.

Hers is a remarkable story of how she has chosen to thrive while balancing her multiple priorities and through the various transitions of her journey.

Let us look at some of the elements of FLAVOUR in the context of Soma's journey.

## A—Tune into Aspiration and make consistent choices

Soma grew up around parents who were in an unhappy, abusive marriage—something that has shaped her profoundly. She left home at fifteen, to study in Pune. 'I was fiercely determined to be financially independent,' she said. That put her on a path to IIMA and Citibank.

While she pursued her corporate banking career relentlessly for a decade, she found herself struggling to balance work and family after her kids were born. Thereafter, as the financial context of her family shifted with Bhavtosh thriving in his career, she found herself in the role of trailing spouse. That caused a gradual shift in her aspirations as well.

A LinkedIn post that she wrote around January 2017 is illuminating. She frames her aspiration as juggling six balls as best as she can.[5] These include: 1) children and husband, 2) painting, 3) work, 4) family and friends, 5) travel and 6) exercise and treks.

More importantly, she frames her aspiration not as a goal but more as the North Star, towards which she is continuously moving by taking baby steps each year.

## L—Make space for what you Love

Art is central to Soma's life, in terms of making space for what she loves.

She uses art as an anchor, a career, a passion, as well as a lens through which to view the world. Even though she used to paint regularly since childhood, art was never a career choice back then, due to it's uncertain financial prospects. 'Forget others, I would never have allowed myself to become an artist,' she said.

Over the years, art has been the harness that held her in place as she climbed her way through life. Once she quit her banking job and moved to Hong Kong, she rediscovered art as a serious pursuit. She used self-coaching to come to terms with her identity as an artist and started painting prolifically. Over the years she has conducted several art exhibitions: across Hong Kong, India and the US, among others.

The effect that art had on her in helping her explore her emotions and facilitate her healing, got her to seek out art therapy as a profession. Art also informs her worldview. 'Art has taught me that there is no perfect painting, that it is in the messiness of the process that growth happens,' she added.

## D—Discern and influence Family context

One dominant theme that emerges in Soma's family context is coming to terms with the domestic violence in her childhood and having closure. It has shaped Soma's choices through life in many ways: be it the drive towards financial independence, the reliance on art as a form of healing, and the journey of healing herself and thereby becoming a therapist herself. 'I now am able to view my experiences from the perspective of gratitude, instead of being the victim,' she said.

The second theme is about navigating the role of trailing spouse and mother, learning to let go of her resentment for a lost corporate career and viewing the shifts as opportunities to discover other facets of herself.

She also speaks about the evolution in her marriage, from being one where she was primarily responsible for the home and kids, to one where her spouse is now a partner who shares responsibility and supports her in her pursuits as she strives to find space for herself in this phase of her life. 'These are messy conversations but, in the messiness, lies the opportunity,' she quipped.

## U—Invest in yoUrself

Soma has invested in herself over the years across various dimensions.

From being somebody who painted for herself, she has invested in her craft and has become an artist whose artwork are bought and displayed by collectors all over the world. She has also invested in formal training at various points in her reinvention journey. She is a certified coach and has a masters in art therapy from New York University. She also invests in her fitness through outdoor treks, walks and yoga. She has also done a lot of solo travel that she says has helped her get in touch with herself.

## VO—Strive to be of Value by seeking/creating Opportunity

Currently, Soma works as a part of the multidisciplinary treatment team at a hospital, treating inpatient adults suffering with psychiatric illnesses. During weekends, she works with children as a part of family counselling services in her local community. During the weekends, she is a creative art therapist at a local hospital that deals with people with deeper psychosis issues, schizophrenia, substance abuse and so on.

She co-founded an award-winning for-profit social enterprise Zaya, based in Mumbai. During her stay in Hong Kong, she became a practicing coach who worked primarily with women. She has also conducted several art exhibitions and sold her art around the world.

## R—Cultivate healthy Relationships

Relationships have played an important role in Soma's life since childhood. 'I gain a lot of joy and nourishment from my relationships,' she said. Her childhood best friend is somebody who she is still close to and travels with.

Despite her many moves, Soma has consistently invested in relationships. Both she and Bhavtosh make the time to call, travel to meet and invite friends over—even on weekdays.

Having friends aged between twenty and seventy means that Soma learns different things from different friendships. 'Anything I am going through, there is somebody who has gone through that, and I can talk to,' she said.

\* \* \*

Soma's story is the journey of a woman who evolves with her changing context to go from a singular view of success to a holistic one that enables her to thrive across multiple dimensions. She has used her multiple constraints and transitions to take charge of her situation instead of playing victim. She has reinvented herself continually, and co-opted her family and her support network so that she can 'juggle the glass balls,' while being kind to herself.

'I strive to be more like a lotus—all petals have to unfurl for the flower to blossom,' she said. There couldn't be a more apt visual description of what striving to play to full potential could mean.

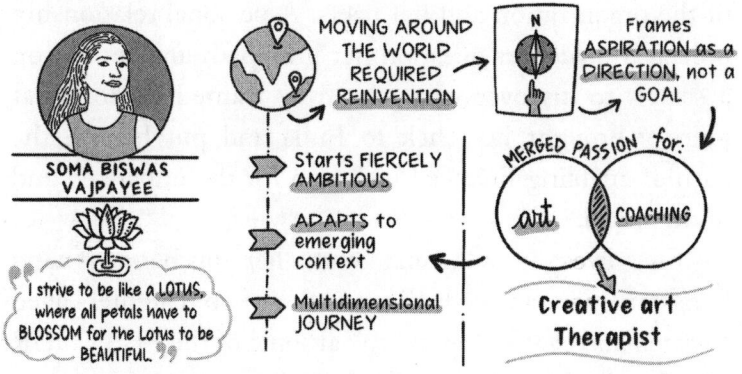

SOMA BISWAS VAJPAYEE

"I strive to be like a LOTUS, where all petals have to BLOSSOM for the Lotus to be BEAUTIFUL."

MOVING AROUND THE WORLD REQUIRED REINVENTION

Frames ASPIRATION as a DIRECTION, not a GOAL

MERGED PASSION for: art COACHING

Starts FIERCELY AMBITIOUS

ADAPTS to emerging context

Multidimensional JOURNEY

Creative art Therapist

## Sucharita Mukherjee—Tuning into Her Aspiration and Purpose to Play to Her Potential

Sucharita is a co-founder at Kaleidofin, a financial inclusion platform, which provides women entrepreneurs in the informal economy with access to capital to power their businesses and, in turn, their families.

A graduate of Lady Shri Ram College, Delhi, and IIM Ahmedabad, Sucharita is a serial entrepreneur who has been obsessed with the idea of financial inclusion for about fifteen years, first at IFMR, and now with Kaleidofin.

Sucharita grew up in an Armed Forces environment with a father who rose to the rank of General in the Indian Army and a working mother. She grew up with 'a lot of trust', 'a belief that she could be anything she wanted to be' and with 'no pressure to excel', she says.

Sucharita started her career as an investment banker in London but found herself misaligned with the values of the organization and her peers. A personal relationship upheaval made her question her life's path and set her on a search to discover what she truly wanted to do. That journey brought her back to India and put her on the path of enabling financial inclusion for the unbanked and underserved.

She lives in Chennai with her husband Anand Sahasranaman, an academic, and their two daughters aged thirteen and eleven. Let us look at some of the FLAVOUR elements in the context of Sucharita's journey.

## A—Tune into Aspiration and make consistent choices

The idea of being aligned to a purpose bigger than the self weaves through Sucharita's life. Starting from childhood, which was spent in an army cantonment, to being influenced by stalwarts like Amartya Sen, the Dalai Lama and Arundhati Roy when they spoke at her undergraduate college, the idea that there is a bigger purpose to life than making money, was consistently reinforced in Sucharita's mind.

After Lady Shri Ram College, she got a brief immersion into rural India when she joined IRMA (Institute of Rural Management, Anand) before she got admission into IIMA. While this was a short window, it planted a seed in her that would germinate much later.

In 2008, after evaluating several opportunities in the development sector, Sucharita chose to join forces with Bindu Ananth and Puneet Gupta (both of whom happened to have been her classmates at IRMA) at IFMR (now Dvara) Holdings.

She was able to bring her experience in capital markets from London and apply it to the context of affordable finance in India. She founded IFMR Capital, a debt capital markets platform for inclusion (now Northern Arc Capital).

Evaluating her actions in hindsight, she mentions that the opportunities that she explored during the two or three years of restlessness were all outside the traditional capitalist career pathways. 'Actions speak louder than words,' she reminisced.

After close to a decade at IFMR, she decided to start a product-led fintech, Kaleidofin, that has, through tech and data, created a product that aims to solve the problem of capital access to the underserved at scale.

Sucharita's aspiration is to take Kaleidofin global. 'There are at least two billion adults in the world who work in the informal sector [who could benefit from capital access],' she says.

## F—Discern and influence Family context

Sucharita was deeply influenced by her parents while growing up, especially in her desire to be financially independent. 'My mother always pursued a job—she was a high school teacher. She drove us around everywhere. My father chipped in at home. You learn from the templates your parents set for you,' she reflected. Her childhood was also filled with music, art, culture and history, and that imbued in her a sense that there is much more to life than the maximization of wealth.

When she had her first child, she was unsure of how to make things work. But her work colleagues, Bindu and Kshama, gave her unwavering support—from conducting meetings in her home to travelling on her behalf, their support made going back to work possible. Having other role models at work such as Dave Wallack, her co-founder who would bring his son Cyrus into meetings, helped her normalize the concept of raising kids while working.

Her husband, Anand Sahasranaman, and his parents have also been pillars of support for Sucharita as she embraced the demanding life of a start-up leader/founder. Anand is an academic and he proactively leans in when Sucharita has to travel for her work. However, Sucharita also mentions that there was a phase when Anand was pursuing his higher studies in the UK, during which she held fort (with the support of the in-laws). She describes her marriage to Anand as a relationship where they have strived to give space to each other to walk their respective paths and have stepped up when it mattered. She underscores the criticality of proactively 'enrolling' the wider family.

## VO—Strive to be of Value by seeking/creating Opportunity

Sucharita and her co-founders started Kaleidofin with the intent of providing women entrepreneurs in the informal sector in India with access to capital.

Sucharita and her co-founders realized that the bridge between capital markets and those in the informal sector was data. Those borrowing from outside of the formal system did not have any mechanism of proving their credit worthiness. Kaleidofin's Ki Score product serves as this bridge.

'The developments in Aadhaar and Tech Stack have opened an opportunity to conceptualize and deliver a technology-led solution to the underbanked consumer,' she said. Ki Score has already enabled the disbursement of over USD 2 billion to women entrepreneurs.

## L—Make space for what you Love

Sucharita is acutely aware of which elements of work she loves. She loves the thrill of creation like building a new product and going to a new market. She confesses that activities like raising money are jobs to be done but don't necessarily bring her joy.

Amidst this intense schedule, she finds time to pursue Indian classical music. She also immensely enjoys travelling with her family immensely.

Sucharita has rediscovered her love for reading, thanks to the pandemic. 'This is one thing I do just for myself,' she says.

## U—Invest in yoUrself

Sucharita is somebody who seems to have listened to her heart from her early years.

She mentioned that she has become more deliberate about her self-awareness journey and has inculcated a daily meditation practice which centres her.

She also speaks about the role of travel (especially solo travel) that helps her get in touch with herself. In the last few years, she speaks about getting her diet and exercise routine in order as well. 'We all need to treat ourselves with the respect we deserve,' she said.

Sucharita has also proactively embraced learning from each of her transitions. When she transitioned to IFMR, she undertook an extensive immersion in some of the rural markets to really understand the needs of the consumer.

When she set up Kaleidofin, she taught herself topics brand new to her: Data science, technology, AI etc.

As she has transitioned contexts, she has kept investing in herself across multiple fronts.

## R—Cultivate healthy Relationships

Sucharita derives energy from some of her close friends from her various cohorts in college. As an accomplished woman leader in Chennai, she is also proactively putting together a community of women leaders who can counsel each other and mentor the next generation of women leaders to emerge from the city. She also mentions that she likes to build friendships when she travels, and these diverse relationships bring richness and learning in her life.

\* \* \*

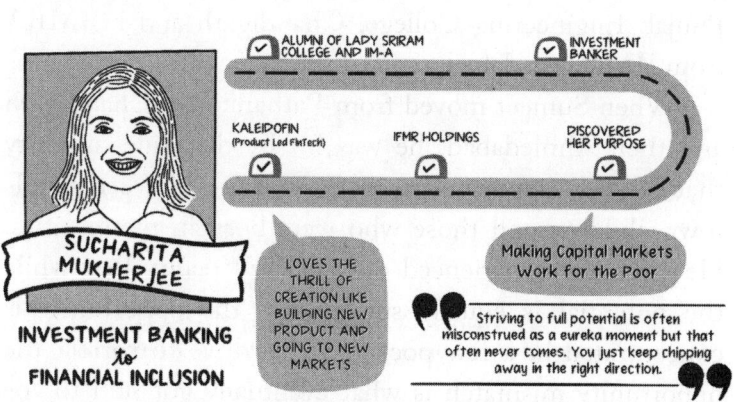

SUCHARITA MUKHERJEE

INVESTMENT BANKING
to
FINANCIAL INCLUSION

ALUMNI OF LADY SRIRAM COLLEGE AND IIM-A

INVESTMENT BANKER

KALEIDOFIN (Product Led FinTech)

IFMR HOLDINGS

DISCOVERED HER PURPOSE

LOVES THE THRILL OF CREATION LIKE BUILDING NEW PRODUCT AND GOING TO NEW MARKETS

Making Capital Markets Work for the Poor

Striving to full potential is often misconstrued as a eureka moment but that often never comes. You just keep chipping away in the right direction.

'Striving to full potential is often misconstrued as a eureka moment but that often never comes. You just keep chipping away in the right direction,' she reflected when asked to describe her approach to playing to her full potential.

## Sumeet Mehta—Discovering his FLAVOUR by Answering his Calling of Re-Imagining Education for 'Bharat'

Sumeet Mehta and his wife Smita Deorah are co-founders of LEAD Group—a school EdTech unicorn (valuation over 1 billion USD) that aims to transform the in-school education experience for millions of kids who go to 'regular' schools in small towns across India.

Sumeet grew up in Pathankot, Punjab to parents who were teachers, thereby imbuing in him a deep respect for the transformative ability of great teaching, and hence, great education. He then pursued his engineering from Punjab Engineering College, Chandigarh and his MBA from IIM Ahmedabad.

When Sumeet moved from Pathankot to Chandigarh and then Ahmedabad, he was hit by the wide disparity that exists in opportunities and awareness between small-town children and those who were born in metro cities. He viscerally experienced our society's reality that while the potential is equally spread out, the opportunity is concentrated in a few pockets. This drive to correct the opportunity mismatch is what eventually got him to co-found LEAD schools.

Sumeet started his post-MBA career in marketing at P&G in Singapore, but in a few years found himself asking how he was really adding value. In 2006, with the support of his wife, he quit P&G to return to India to do something in the space of education. He spent five years with Zee Learn to understand the education sector and then quit to start LEAD with his wife and co-founder Smita Deorah.

Sumeet lives in Mumbai, with Smita, his mother and two children—a daughter aged sixteen and a son aged fourteen.

Let us look at some of the elements of FLAVOUR in the context of Sumeet's journey.

## A—Tune into Aspiration and make consistent choices

While Sumeet walked a predictable path post IIMA for five to six years, he started tuning into what gave him energy during a six-month sabbatical in 2005. While he experimented with a few things, it was conducting a summer camp 'Beyond Books' for school kids along with his parents and Smita, that served as a clarifying experience. 'I had so much fun, and so did the kids, that I decided I wanted to work with children from kindergarten to class 12.'

The initial aspiration for Sumeet and Smita was just to ensure children in at least one village school would get access to the same education quality as children in elite city schools. However, as their business model evolved, and their ability to make an impact multiplied, their aspiration shifted as well.

'It is heartbreaking that 270 million students in India are not going to grow to their full potential. I feel I would have left the world better than I inherited it if I could help children become capable adults, responsible citizens and good human beings through a joyful schooling experience,' he articulated.

Today, there is the sobering realization that given the size of the problem, it may not get solved in their lifetime. Their aspiration has shifted again therefore from 'solving the problem to creating the vehicle to solve the problem' by building LEAD as a values-driven organization.

### F—Discern and influence Family context

Sumeet says his father, an English teacher, was a powerful influence in his life, giving him a sense of what a good teacher could do and his passion for doing something in the education space.

Having read *Rich Dad, Poor Dad* at a young age, Sumeet and Smita decided on a basic savings number they must reach before they could pursue what they loved. 'Our needs are simple, we just prioritized maintaining the life we currently lead, and ensuring we had enough savings to give our children a good education.' Being on a sound financial footing helped Sumeet and Smita build for the long run without having to worry about staying afloat.

Sumeet and his partner Smita are co-founders not just at LEAD but also in life. Given their hectic schedules, they are mindful that they need to step up and cover for each other at work or at home as the situation demands. 'Our marriage is not a 1.5:0.5,' he said, referring to the load balance at home. 'Neither is it a 1:1,' he was quick to add. 'It is possibly closer to a 1.1:0.9,' acknowledging the slight additional load Smita might be carrying.

Sumeet and Smita demonstrate a deep level of trust and mutual respect that permeates through their world of work and otherwise.

## VO—Strive to be of Value by seeking/creating Opportunity

The journey of LEAD from one school to 9000 and continuing—is a fascinating one—one that started with trying to be of value to a handful of children to evolving the business model that serves millions.

Sumeet (and Smita) have done this by honing the true value the LEAD system provides to students—pedagogy and improving learning outcomes. In doing so, they took a conscious call to step back from the parts of running a school that do not enable this value, investments in infrastructure and school operations. Their clarity on the value they want to provide has empowered them to create an asset-light-school in a box system which is easy to deploy and easy to scale, without compromising on learning outcomes.

In their case, focusing on value has unlocked a very large market opportunity for LEAD resulting in them becoming a unicorn.

## U—Invest in yoUrself

Sumeet has done significant inner work over the years. From going to therapy to overcome the complex emotions he wrestled with after losing his dad, to going to the Landmark forum to understand the disabling patterns and blind spots running his life, to taking a sabbatical, to going to Vipassana meditation, Sumeet has deeply invested in self-awareness.

He has also invested in learning about education in formal and informal ways. He and Smita have attended programmes at Harvard Graduate School of Education and visited over 200-300 schools across the world to learn about best practices in education. As avid readers, he and Smita are constantly reading about learning, brain development and the latest in the field of education and applying that in their work.

Post-Covid, Sumeet has also strived to bring his physical fitness back on track and has institutionalized that in his organization.

## L—Make space for what you Love

Sumeet's work energizes him completely. It gives him what he calls 'gladness of heart'. 'At this point in time, I am not doing anything that drains me. My work and my love are the same and that is a blessing,' he acknowledged.

## R—Invest in Relationships

Sumeet refers to the four chambers of his heart and speaks about four domains that he focuses on—us (referring to him and Smita), kids, parents and LEAD. He recognizes that the life of an entrepreneur is demanding, and that they are going after an aspirational vision. He mentions that as a result, he hasn't had as much time socializing and meeting friends (as much as he would like to). However, making this a deliberate choice has helped him feel comfortable with this decision.

\* \* \*

Sumeet recollects that his father used to say that one needs to have a 'divine discontentment with the status quo'. He has tried to use that as a compass to find direction. When asked about what matters more, the journey or the destination, he calls out a third element: 'the partner'. Smita and Sumeet are a couple that are savouring the journey towards a noble destination that involves changing the lives of millions of children in India.

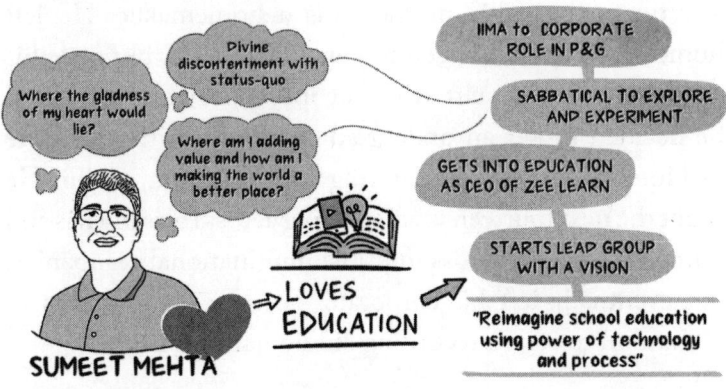

## Vineet Panchhi—Wearing Multiple Hats and Tuning into What Gives Energy to Live an Authentic Life

'How do you catch a cloud and pin it down? How do you find a word that describes Maria?' these are phrases that are used to describe Julie Andrews' character in *The Sound of Music*. Vineet is one of those breeds. Just like his name 'Panchhi', which means a free bird, it is hard to pin him down. However, in the coming paragraphs, I will take a stab at it.

Vineet Panchhi wears multiple hats of poet, storyteller, activist, communications consultant, voiceover artist, musician and TEDx speaker. He is the founder of Word of Mouth Media—a communications and advertising agency based in Dehradun. He has also founded the Jai Hind Project, which shines the spotlight on everyday heroes.

Vineet grew up in Machhi Bazaar, Dehradun in a middle-class home where his father worked with the government and his mother was a homemaker. He left home at the age of sixteen to join a local band, but once his school classmates started to get into NDA and the IITs, he decided to get an undergrad degree from the Institute of Hotel Management Catering and Nutrition, Delhi. He spent the next fourteen years growing across roles in sales and human resources, across multiple multinational companies, but eventually left his corporate job in 2009 to return to Dehradun to start a recording studio with his uncle.

'I divide my life into before 2009 and after 2009,' he said. He discovered his purpose over time and after trying and incubating a few initiatives around media, music, corporate communications, voiceover and filmmaking, he is now running a crusade titled Jai Hind Project, an ambitious initiative that is out to give India the heroes that it ought to celebrate than the ones that are currently served to the public's consciousness.

Let us look at some of the elements of FLAVOUR in the context of Vineet's journey.

## F—Discern and influence Family context

Vineet grew up in Dehradun and has vivid memories of his father's alcohol problem that required him to be the 'man of the house' right from when he was a teenager. That got him to subconsciously imbibe the idea that he needed to make a lot of money to support his family. This shaped his career after his undergrad, for fourteen years, as he moved from job to job—in the Delhi NCR region— lured by higher salaries, working for companies such as Nirula's, Reebok, Bose, GECIS, Carlson Wagonlit changing roles—but growing in his career along the way.

Moving back to his hometown, Dehradun and giving up a steady job, caused stresses and strains that eventually took a toll on his marriage. He and his wife are separated now and have moved on and are happy in their respective new relationships. He speaks about how his view on pursuing his passions has changed over time to include relationships as well.

'My partner uses the term PIC—partnership, intimacy, companionship—to describe how good or optimal your relationships are. Partnership is being invested in your partner's success as much as your own, intimacy is feeling emotionally and otherwise safe with your partner, and companionship is enjoying some of the same things together. I use PIC now across work relationships as well,' he said.

## A—Tune into Aspiration and make consistent choices

The real shift in his aspiration came about after he returned to Dehradun. 'My relationship with money changed after I moved back,' he said.

He now defines his aspiration as enabling smart young people from his hometown to build skills and find work locally without having to migrate to bigger cities. 'Over 200 people have passed through our stables, and I am proud to say, nobody has had to move to find work,' he added.

His other large aspiration is to shift the conversation around role models with the Jai Hind Project, an initiative that consumes him today. 'All our billboards have cricketers or movie stars,' he laments.

'The goal is to also bring back empathy in our society' he said, adding, 'The younger generation is growing up in a bubble and does not know how a milkman, a shopkeeper, a postman lives their life . . . There are everyday heroes all around us and we need to shine the spotlight on them.'

## L—Making space for what you Love

Vineet's love for music began as a young boy when he was influenced by his uncle to listen to bands like Led Zeppelin and Pink Floyd. He joined his uncle's band and got great joy from performing on stage with him in his high school years.

Ever since his return to Dehradun in 2008, Vineet has strived to follow his heart and pursue what he truly loved (at times to his commercial detriment). He now finds expression through some of the work he has done that includes doing voice-overs, directing ad films for companies, recording jingles, running his company and through the Jai Hind Project.

'Even now, I earn less than I used to in my corporate career, but I can never go back to that. Life is too short to wait for one day to finally focus on one's passion,' he shared thoughtfully.

## VO—Strive to be of Value by seeking/creating Opportunity

Vineet is somebody who has been extremely fluid about his professional identity and has donned many hats over the years. He has used his passion for music, poetry and storytelling and married that to his people skills, business understanding, empathy and his adaptability to monetize his capabilities across a vast array of careers in sales, human resources, operations, training, communication and advertising, among others.

## U—Invest in yoUrself

After a few years of Sales and related roles post his hotel management degree in IHM, Vineet decided to do an executive programme from XLRI – Xavier School of Management which opened the door to HR and leadership development.

Along the way, he also got inspired by Professor Philip Zimbardo who was known for his controversial experiment in 1971—the Stanford Prison Experiment which later became a collective social experiment called the Heroic Imagination Project, a non-profit research and education organization dedicated to training people to act in more heroic ways. Vineet is a Level 2 trainer in this approach. In this journey, Vineet stumbled across Matt Langdon's quote: 'The opposite of a hero is not a villain, it is a bystander.'[6] This quote hit him hard and that led him to start the Jai Hind Project. 'I used to express my anger with the way things are by getting into scraps. This helps me channel that as a force for change.'

Vineet's journey has also been one of living a life of integrity, aware of his hypocrisies and what drives him and his beliefs. He refers to the candid feedback from near and dear in a safe space as a key contributor to his growth (his current partner, dad, sister, daughter and friends).

## R—Cultivate healthy Relationships

Vineet operates from the heart and has built deep authentic relationships over the years. His LinkedIn profile speaks about treasuring the time with his friends from college. He has deep connections in Dehradun where he has made a difference in the journey of many individuals through the media incubator that he runs—Word of Mouth Media. He is also a poet and has a popular YouTube channel that has spawned new relationships and speaking opportunities across the country. Vineet is an exemplar of the approach— you show up in a certain way and your tribe emerges!

When you ask him about his inspiration, he quotes his mentor Ambar Kharbandaji in Hindi.

*Mushkil ko samajhne ka tareeka nikal aata,*
*Tum baat to karte, koi rasta nikal aata*
*Mere liye ae dost itna hi bahut tha,*
*Jaise tujhe socha tha, tu waise nikal aata*


The way to understand the difficulty would have emerged,
If only you had spoken, a solution would have come forth.
For me, my friend, it would have been enough,
If you had turned out just as I had imagined you.

This piece refers to the criticality of healthy communication to solve intractable problems. Through the Jai Hind Project, Vineet is on a crusade to get the country getting to know and communicate with each other!

\* \* \*

'Don't ask what the world needs. Ask what makes you come alive, and go do it. Because what the world needs is people who have come alive.' This quote by Howard Thurman captures the essence of Vineet's approach to life.

## Chapter Synthesis

Each of the journeys presented above is layered and complex. It would be inappropriate to capture decades of experiences and choices into a couple of bullets. Instead, if any of the stories spoke to you and you would like to know more, we would urge you to tune into the detailed conversations I had with these six people where they outlined their approach to how they got here.

You can go to the link https://bit.ly/Flavourfullife or scan the QR code below for accessing it on YouTube.

# THEMES FROM
# FLAVOURFUL LIVES

Our FLAVOUR keeps evolving – requires rediscovering as we progress

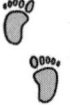

Aspiration can be defined as a BIG goal or small steps in the direction of who you want 'to be'

Each starts at a different point on FLAVOUR journey. If you are stuck, tuning into your aspiration may be a good place to start

No journey is a straight line – involves significant twists and turns

Working on our self-awareness helps get to where we want to go

Some are passion led and some are purpose led. There is no right answer. We need to stay true to what tugs us.

Each of them demonstrates a sense of agency and taking charge of their journey than playing victim to the situation

Many love their work but some find things that give them joy outside work.

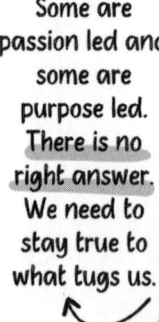

Each invidividual navigates transitions with a sense of deliberate intent

# 8

# Meta-Skills for a FLAVOUR-ful Life

*It's my life, it's now or never*
*I ain't gonna live forever*
*I just want to live while I'm alive*
*It's my life*
*My heart is like the open highway*
*Like Frankie[1] said I did it my way*
*I just wanna live while I'm alive*
*It's my life*

—Lyrics: Jon Bon Jovi, Richie Sambora and Max
Martin; song: 'It's My Life'; singer: Bon Jovi

We now have more than eight billion human beings inhabiting this planet, each one unique in their way. Whether it is our DNA, place and circumstances of birth, styles of parenting, nature of sibling context, life experiences, education, relationships and so on—these elements are different. We might have the temptation to compare ourselves to our schoolmates, college mates, work peers etc. but when we scratch the surface it doesn't take long to discover the uniqueness of each of our journeys. Even twins with identical DNAs at birth are shown to have different life outcomes[2] because of epigenetics which is known to be the mechanism by which environmental changes alter the behaviour of our genes. If twins at birth experience can have very different life outcomes, suffice it to say that we all can assume that we are on a journey that is uniquely ours. The corollary to this is that each one of us, therefore, has to figure out what FLAVOUR-ful means given our unique life context. As Frank Sinatra says, each one of us has to discover/craft what 'my way' means for us.

In the previous chapter, we saw six disparate journeys of individuals who I believe are striving to play to their full potential. In this chapter, I present what I believe are some of the underlying skill sets, mindsets and mental models we might need to proactively architect and live a FLAVOUR-ful life.

## Embrace Your Uniqueness

*Keeping Up with the Joneses*, a comic strip created by Arthur R. Momand, ran between 1913 and 1940 in *New York World*. It depicted the experiences of the McGinis family, who struggle to keep up with their neighbours. While this comic strip was created about a century ago, it speaks to a universal human tendency which has only been further amplified with the prevalence of social media in our lives. When I overlay this tendency with the world of career pathways exploding with newer and newer possibilities coming up every day, this tendency is a recipe for a mental health catastrophe. We first need to acknowledge that each one of us is unique in terms of who we are and the context we find ourselves in and build from there.

I must confess that I was like the McGinis for a long time in my life where I tried to keep up with my peers (schoolmates, batchmates from my undergrad and postgrad schools, peers at McKinsey and Egon Zehnder, neighbours and so on). It put me on a path of achievement and accomplishment but it also led to tremendous levels of insecurity, unhappiness and time-poverty as I went about my life at McKinsey and Egon Zehnder. Over the last eight-plus years, only when I have attempted to embrace my uniqueness and what matters to me, I feel I could start taking baby steps towards building a FLAVOUR-ful life.

A key element of uniqueness is around the notion of discovering our skill stack. Very often, we look at our career as a summation of the various roles we have held. But when we look at our unique skills and traits and other capabilities with a creative lens, interesting possibilities emerge.

Papa CJ has successfully combined his diverse skills and experiences across comedy, business and leadership to build a unique niche for himself. After an MBA from Oxford and a consulting job in London, he took an unconventional path by venturing into stand-up comedy in

2004. With over 700 shows in the UK, he returned to India and became one of the pioneers the stand-up industry here.

For the past two decades, CJ has straddled the worlds of comedy and executive coaching, leveraging his expertise at the intersection of creativity, communication, humour, storytelling, business and human interaction. His signature programmes, *A Comedian's Guide to Communication Strategy* and *Naked Leadership*, demonstrate his ability to integrate these diverse domains. In the former, he helps businesses and executives enhance their storytelling by applying strategies and tools used by professional comedians. In the latter, based on his stand-up show and book *Naked*, he guides leaders and organizations to lead with authenticity and vulnerability to improve trust and drive cross-functional collaboration.

CJ's journey highlights the potential of recognizing and creatively combining our unique capabilities and experiences across different fields, unlocking new opportunities for growth and impact. He also demonstrates how we can be fluid across the various domains we inhabit and lead a multi-dimensional life. A key element of a multi-dimensional life is tuning into what we really want across the various dimensions. Something that nobody teaches us.

## Be Aware of Your Aspiration Across Your Identities

Very often, when I see some of my friends take stock of their lives, I see them resorting to looking at the quantum of their tangible assets: their net worth, the value of their home and so on. I realize that for us to lead a full life and play to our full potential, we need to think of ourselves as investors of a slightly different kind. Just like one has a portfolio of assets, we need to imagine a portfolio of various identities that we need to invest our time and attention in and ensure that the portfolio is well-diversified across the various domains of life. Soma Biswas Vajpayee (featured in the previous chapter) speaks about how she sets an annual intention for six domains of her life and chips away at them in a deliberate way.

I have found it useful to get my clients to embark on an exercise to take stock of their various identities and their aspirations for each element of their identity. The exercise[3] requires you to find a quiet spot for half a day or a full day where you are not distracted, and you don't have any devices pinging and disturbing you.

Imagine yourself five years out. Not ten years, not one year, five years.

First, you think of the various identities that matter to you across the various domains of life (say spouse, son, musician, runner, professional and so on). I notice that very often we gravitate to our professional identity as a default. This is the time to go broad and look at the various roles you play in your life and the associated identities. The key is to give adequate importance to the various elements of FLAVOUR as you think about the various identities.

According to Lloyd Reeb[4] (🎤), who has studied midlife transitions, this is also a time to reflect on dormant themes that have been smouldering under wet blankets over the years because you didn't have the time, money or other resources to pursue a certain passion. We don't have to be constrained by the identities we currently carry. Now is the time to say 'can I invest in a pursuit(s) so that in five years, there is a possibility that a new identity emerges?' It could be around a hobby, a social impact initiative or a fitness challenge. Write down the list of five to ten identities that you care about on one page.

Now, for each of the identities, try and find an adjective that you would like to attach to that identity at the end of five years. For instance, a 'loving spouse', 'caring son', 'soulful musician', 'competitive long-distance runner', 'ambitious professional' and so on . . . you get the drift. One identity and one additional word which qualifies the kind of person you want to be in that domain of your life. Don't rush this. Take your time. Once you are done with this, write down each of these two-word combinations on a separate page. If you have ten identities, take ten sheets of paper and write the two words on top of each sheet of paper. One page would have a caring parent, another would have a loving spouse, the next would have an ambitious professional and so on.

Now take each page and ask yourself 'why' multiple times. Why is that important to you? Stay with one page for a few minutes. As long as it takes. Don't rush the process. This is like going down an iceberg. When I did this exercise recently, one of the adjective-identity pairs I wrote down was to be a nurturing parent. Here is how traversing down the base of the iceberg looked for me on that one particular dimension when I did this process the last time.

**Level 1:** I want to be a nurturing parent. *Why is that important?*

**Level 2:** It is critical for the kids to grow up with a sense of emotional security. *Why is that important?*

**Level 3:** It is a messy, complex world and there is a chance of the kids getting into a negative loop if things don't go to plan for them. *Why is that important?*

**Level 4:** Given the proliferation of devices, social media comparisons and the uncertainties involved in journeys and pathways, they could end up being unhappy in life and possibly have mental health issues. *Why is that important?*

**Level 5:** Happiness is something I wish for the kids. A life of accomplishment and success without inner happiness is hollow and I wouldn't want them to be in that place.

I hope you were able to make sense of how this works. If you do the exercise yourself, you will initially discover some feelings and emotions you have around that identity. As you ask 'why' and go deeper, you will find that you unearth your values and beliefs. If you go deeper, you are likely to find some basic needs you are trying to meet or fears you are trying to avoid. There is no right answer here. The idea is to just stay with the page and go as deep as you can till you get a sense that you have gotten to the bottom of that iceberg. Not only does this exercise provide perspective on what it means to you to be a parent, it also acts as a mirror to your beliefs, fears and values. You then move to the next page, continue this exercise and go down the bottom of the iceberg and so on till you complete all the pages across the various identities.

After you go through the process of building awareness of your aspirations across the various identities, make a personal declaration for what you are committing to in the journey along each of the identities so that it becomes a self-regulating mechanism when you swing too far in one of the aspects of life. Very often, when we get consumed by the rough and tumble of daily life we lose track of what our portfolio allocation ought to be and end up focusing on the obvious elements of the portfolio like work and ignoring the rest. And that divergence over time can lead to dissonance.

Sometimes, we might swing to the other extreme. Without having a clear direction, we might not have the courage to say 'no' to 100s of unimportant distractions, while learning to focus on the handful important ones. This might make us feel directionless.

Doing the adjective–identity exercise can give us a lighthouse to swim towards during the high seas of midlife. Without it, we might be a bit adrift across the oceans, lacking in direction. However, there is a way in which we can engage with the various dimensions which do not stretch us and give us a healthy return on investment on our time and energy.

## Osmosis and Four-Way Wins

We often think of life as consisting of two elements—work and everything outside of work, which often is strangely referred to as 'life', thereby leading to the term 'work-life' balance. I found this taxonomy inaccurate, incomplete and unsettling for many years till I came across the work of Prof. Stew Friedman (🎤) at Wharton. He speaks about four domains of life—self, work, home and community. He speaks about how we all need to tune into what each of these dimensions means to us. He urges us to engage with each domain in a way that energizes us and helps us bring that energy to the other domains. He also goes on to say that this is not a zero-sum game where we are trading off across various domains. He urges us to be smart about how we engage with these domains.

Stew uses the term four-way wins to suggest that if we are thoughtful and deliberate, we can pursue all four domains with lesser effort. Rather than treat the four compartments as water-tight, if we allow osmosis, it might throw up interesting possibilities. Let me illustrate that with an episode from 2013.

In the spirit of improving my fitness, cajoled by a few friends, I ended up signing up for the Mumbai Half Marathon. To prepare, I signed up with a running group called Striders and trained with them for a few months leading up to the run. In the process I involved some of my colleagues from Egon Zehnder and raised funds for the Salaam Bombay Foundation—an NGO that works with children who have tobacco addiction and helps them lead a healthy life. It turned out that I was one of their highest fundraisers that year and their brand ambassador was the Bollywood singer Shaan. As a thank-you gesture, they got the high fundraisers to go to Shaan's studio and record a song. When the day came, I took my wife, my three-year-old daughter and my sister and we went to Shaan's studio in Bandra and recorded a couple of songs along with him. I sang 'It's the Time to Disco' from *Kal Ho Naa Ho* and my daughter sang 'Edelweiss' while I strummed the guitar. Those videos and photos that we took that day are priceless and we cherish the memories for a long time to come. When I reflect, I feel that this was a case where I feel I was able to work on my health by running, developed some new friendships through Striders, strengthened work relationships by involving my colleagues and registering some of them for the Mumbai run, made a difference to kids who were addicted to tobacco and also created some memories for my family.

Stew calls these 4-way wins where we do things in a way so that we kill multiple birds with one stone. Now, not every situation lends itself to a four-way win, but I have become more deliberate to structure things in a way so that I can kill two, three or four birds with a stone rather than one stone each. It is worth pausing and asking yourself the question—what does the portfolio allocation of time look like for you across these four dimensions? Where do you see an opportunity for rebalancing and fine-tuning? Can you do things in a way so that you can engineer two-way, three-way or four-way wins? This approach can help us get more juice out of the limited and perishable time we have at our disposal.

However, this also requires some adjustment in our mindset and mental models and for us to be intentional in managing the tension across a few areas we discuss next.

## Walking the Tightropes Intentionally

Leading a FLAVOUR-ful life requires us to prioritize across multiple domains and navigate the tension between them. It is not about swinging too far on either side. It is often about finding a middle path creatively while balancing one's priorities, akin to a tightrope artist.

### Unidimensional optimizing and multi-dimensional satisficing

When one aspect of our life is going well, we end up pouring our heart and soul into that element of our life and neglecting the others. If we are doing well in our career (VO), there might be a tendency to focus on U (investing in ourselves) but ignore F (family) or R (relationships) or L (finding space for your passion) where there is no immediate return on our investment. We all know our share of corporate athletes who often don't have adequate time (do not make adequate time to be precise) for their families or their passions or their other relationships. At the other end of the spectrum might be homemakers who might be pouring their energies into taking care of the family (F) and invest in relationships (R) but often don't think enough about being of value to the world outside (VO) that leads to self-worth issues that can further lead to strained familial relationships.

A key element of this is acknowledging the 'good enough' point where the additional investment in that dimension is not worth the benefit of spending that time and attention on a different domain. That additional hour in the workplace in the evening when compared to sending kids to bed, the early morning golf round with friends against having time to catch up on your sleep, that additional hour spent playing poker versus dinner with the spouse. Economists use the term 'diminishing marginal utility', in the context of consumption. It states that each additional unit of gain leads to decreasing subjective value. In simple terms, the first scoop of ice-cream could give us a lot of happiness compared to none. But the tenth scoop may not bring that much additional joy compared to the ninth scoop (it might even make it worse).

This is not to suggest that we go for mediocrity in all domains and do a 'good enough' job everywhere. I have been in advisory services all my working life. I notice that the long hours spent in the office are often not to service the client but to service our insecurity![5] My submission here is that if we look hard enough, there are many places where we are allocating time and attention to the twentieth scoop with no tangible outcome and if we can redirect that to some of the undernourished elements of our life, we could live a much richer life. A pre-requisite here for us is situational awareness as we go through life, something we discuss in the next section.

## Building habits and being aware

I notice that very often we develop healthy habits to get through life. But when taken to an extreme, it could mean that we are not being intentional every moment. Devdutt Pattanaik (🎤) speaks about the fact that being completely habit-driven taken to the extreme means that we are being conditioned to a certain way of doing things (like Pavlov's dog) without being clear about the 'why' or being present to the changes in your environment. Going for a three-hour morning run is great for discipline but if you are not getting adequate sleep, or not eating well, or you are under the weather, being dogmatic about pursuing the habit can lead to burnout or a health event that could bring your life to a standstill.

I notice that there are many micro-choices during the day and the week where one has to be aware of the various moving parts in FLAVOUR to ensure that we prioritize and reprioritize our time and attention and not fall victim to our habit in a certain area of our life which we can run on autopilot. This is where the internal and external self-awareness pursuits that we discussed earlier in Section B of the book and the identity exercise  we discussed earlier in this chapter become relevant.

Driving coherence in the FLAVOUR framework is not about a set of one-time static choices. It consists of hundreds of micro-choices you make in the day which lead to coherence. If you see a person walk on a tightrope from point A to point B, it might seem simple from the outside. What you don't observe is that inside the seemingly calm exterior is a set of core muscles coupled with extreme awareness which together ensure the balance as the person walks the rope. I believe there is something similar at play when we strive for coherence in our FLAVOUR. Our awareness becomes our set of core muscles that drive coherence as we get pulled in different directions.

## Having a view of profit and loss and balance sheet

Playing to full potential as a long game also requires us to develop a healthy balance of orientation towards performance and health. Some of the dimensions of FLAVOUR (especially VO) can drag us to double down on performance because the short-term returns are very visible. If you are hitting it out of the park as a partner in a consulting firm or delivering strong shareholder returns as a CEO, the tendency would be to double down on it and reap the rewards. That is where F, L, U and R are a healthy counterbalance to keep in mind. Spending time with family, having space for something you truly love and investing in yourself and relationships. These often act as the strong roots on which the tree of performance can stand and grow further.

As we go through our journey, we must have a healthy bifocal lens,[6] one portion that focuses on the performance today and another portion that ensures that you develop the tangible and intangible assets to help you deliver the performance over the long game of life.

## Solving for time and money

Ashley Whillans[7](🎙) has researched how people trade-off between money and time and how that links with happiness, success and other elements of life. As part of her research, she looks at two categories of people that could be loosely called Taylors and Morgans (or Teresas and Michelles as the case might be). Taylor is somebody who values their time more than the money and someone of that profile is willing to give up money to have more free time. Morgan, on the other hand, values their money more than their free time. They are willing to give up time to have more money.

Her research suggests that Taylors often end up being happier than Morgans. She goes on to say that however counter-intuitive it might be, Taylors might even end up making more money than the Morgans. That is possibly because they truly try to focus on what brings them joy and 'flow' and therefore make choices which put them on a path where they can 'play' to potential rather than try to work their way up there.

When I look around, I notice that people end up prioritizing money much more than time and that can come in the way of leading a full life. Playing to full potential, I believe, requires a combination of solving for a healthy level of abundance of time and money. This is where tuning into our needs and wants and discerning the 'good enough' point for money can help.

I notice that a big pre-requisite for this is for us to tune into our heart and what it is saying. We often spend too much time thinking about what is rational and what our head is saying. We often don't tune into how we are feeling as much as we should. That requires us to build our heart muscle.

## Cultivating Our Heart

We often come across advice about heeding to your heart at various points in time. Amish Tripathi (🎤), when he discusses the transition from being a leader in the financial services industry to the world of writing, speaks about tuning to the heart and head for different things. 'Use your heart to decide the destination but use your mind to plot the journey,' he said. Sumeet Mehta (profiled in the previous chapter) speaks about how, at various points in time, he has asked himself 'where does the gladness of my heart lie' and that has shown him the way forward. I realize that the heart is a muscle (literally and metaphorically) and very often I notice that the leaders I come in touch with do not do enough to develop that muscle. A lot of our education and professional training is often about cultivating the head, often leaving the heart behind. In a lot of these instances, it is not that the individual doesn't want to listen to their heart. It is just that the muscle is underdeveloped.

Three approaches come to mind in this context of developing the heart muscle.

Firstly, consider having some art in your life. I believe that the heart and art are closely connected. Given the economics of pursuing art as a career, most of us don't walk that path. In a country like India, where to get through examinations you have to be tunnel-visioned and often go all in, several of us sacrificed our co-curricular activities and focused just on academics. As a result, I have noticed that several leaders in the corporate world end up having a low exposure to art. When it comes to pursuing hobbies, they often end up pursuing a sport or running as it also takes care of their health.

The Late Sir Ken Robinson said that music often touches parts of the soul that words don't. I have empirically noticed that there is much truth to this. Music is just one of the many pathways. It could be dancing, painting, cooking, gardening, theatre and much more. Anything that gets you to focus on how you feel rather than what you think. The ideal would be to pursue it in some shape or form. If not, the next best is to have exposure to art—go to concerts, painting galleries, theatre, stand-up shows and more.

Secondly, I suggest you consider bringing in some awe in the rhythm of your life. I first learnt about awe in my conversation with Prof. Raj Raghunathan[8] (🎙) who spoke about the link between awe and happiness. The broad definition of awe is the feeling you experience when you are in the presence of something much bigger than you. Something that gives you goosebumps. This could be

watching the sunrise, seeing a movie like *Avatar* in IMAX
3D with spectacular special effects, seeing your child speak
their first word, watching a bird assemble a nest in your
balcony, catching a cheetah chasing a gazelle at the Maasai
Mara or gazing into the sky and looking at the stars. I get
goosebumps each time I listen to a certain set of songs
from Ilayaraja, the music legend from Tamil Nadu. Some
of his songs connect me to my childhood and make me
pause in my tracks. Very often, I notice that we get into
the trap of doing things that give us a return on investment
of some sort and that very soon leads to a dreary existence
with a lot of material possessions but without emotional
richness. Awe keeps our ego in check and nourishes the
heart muscle by getting us to focus on the sheer beauty of
the things around us just the way they are. When we live
in concrete urban jungles, it can be hard to have awe in our
lives. We all need to be deliberate about it. Dacher Keltner,
in his book *Awe*, discusses the value of this and multiple
strategies around it if you wish to dig into greater detail.

A question worth asking yourself in this context is:
'When was the last time you got goosebumps?' What was
the context in which it happened? Maybe try and get more
of those moments into your life.

The third thought here is to consider engaging in some
form of philanthropy if you have not already. I feel it puts
life in perspective, builds gratitude and develops the heart.
While a lot of us might be doing work in the space of
social impact, occasionally going to the ground and seeing
where the rubber meets the road can help build the heart

muscle. I notice that very often people frame philanthropy as their contribution to the world around them. In my instance, I feel I have gained much more than what I have given through my short journey of philanthropy through Antarang Foundation, Akanksha Foundation and Social Venture Partners. This journey has helped me develop gratitude, build perspective and most importantly, played a role in developing the heart muscle.

There are many other approaches to building the heart muscle but these three just happen to be the ones that seem to work for me. The limited point I want to make here is listening to the heart is often a lot more about developing the heart muscle than developing the listening capability.

This chapter discusses some of the mindsets and capabilities we need to lead a FLAVOUR-ful life. It treats life as a 'going concern'. But the reality is that the wheel of life keeps spinning and we need to discover our new FLAVOUR especially when seasons and circumstances change.

The skills we need to be FLAVOUR-ful on an ongoing basis can be quite different from the skills and mindsets we need to navigate a transition to a new normal. It is a bit like the distinction between fine motor skills and gross motor skills. Both are required for our daily lives but having one does not guarantee the other. The two require different kinds of training. If this chapter was about being a meticulous goldsmith, the next one is about effective black-smithery for us to rediscover a new normal as we go through a transition.

## Contextual Audio Snippets from the Podcast

**Audio Clip 8.1:** Lloyd Reeb on how identities can be born

**Audio Clip 8.2:** Stew Friedman on four domains of life—self, work, home and community

**Audio Clip 8.3:** Devdutt Pattanaik on habits and awareness

**Audio Clip 8.4:** Amish Tripathi on head vs heart when it comes to decision-making

**Audio Clip 8.5:** Raj Raghunathan on the role of awe in inspiring us

**Audio Clip 8.6:** Ashley Whillans on Taylors (people who prioritize time) and Morgans (People who prioritize money) and the link between happiness and financial outcomes

# META SKILLS FOR A FLAVOURFUL LIFE

## BE SMART ENGAGING IN DIFFERENT DOMAINS OF LIFE

Integrated view of different domains helps us frame two-way, three-way or four-way goals

## GET COMFORTABLE TO WALK TIGHT ROPES

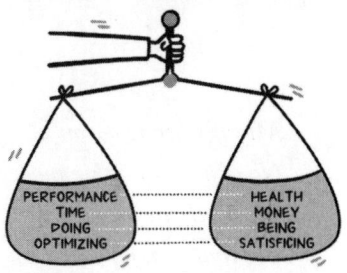

PERFORMANCE
TIME
DOING
OPTIMIZING

HEALTH
MONEY
BEING
SATISFICING

## WE NEED TO EMBRACE OUR UNIQUENESS

We have UNIQUE skill set, capabilities and relationships that can be used creatively in our INDIVIDUALIZED context

## BE AWARE OF ASPIRATION ACROSS VARIOUS IDENTITIES

Awareness acts as a compass that shows us the way to allocate our time and attention as we walk our path

## STRIVE TO CULTIVATE YOUR HEART MUSCLE

Have some element of art in your life

Put yourself in situations where you experience awe

Consider engaging in some form of time philantrophy

# 9

# Rediscovering Our FLAVOUR of the Season

*Musafir hoon yaaron*
*Na ghar hai na thikana*
*Mujhe chalte jaana hai*
*Bas chalte jaana*

I am a traveller, dear friends
Don't have a home or a base
I need to keep walking
Just keep walking!

—Lyrics: Anand Bakshi;
movie: *Parichay*; singer: Kishore Kumar

'Flavour of the month' originated as a marketing tactic used by ice cream sellers in the US around the 1940s. Over time, this phrase transformed into a widely recognized idiom, extending its meaning beyond ice cream to denote anything temporarily in vogue.

While a month might be too short in a person's life for the flavour to change, I do believe that we all go through seasons in our lives which seem to shift every few years, I have found that playing to full potential involves tuning into the season we are in and in crafting the FLAVOUR that is fit for purpose.

I notice that three broad elements govern the change in season we experience and precipitate the need for us to rediscover our FLAVOUR.

*Life transitions around us*: While there are many gradual shifts as time elapses in terms of these are sudden changes in circumstances with time that require us to reassess our FLAVOUR. If you are a working professional, this could be retiring from the workforce when you turn sixty. For a homemaker, it could be children leaving the home to pursue studies.

*Choices we (or people around us) make:* This includes choices that have an impact on the time, money and energy we have at our disposal for various elements of our lives. On the personal front, this could mean choices around marriage/divorce and children and on the professional front, this could be joining or quitting jobs, plunging into entrepreneurship and so on.

*Events that happen to us:* While we might seem to think that we have a semblance of control and predictability over life, some events could change the context completely. This could be the death of a loved one or a health episode in our life, being laid off from one's company or crossing the point of financial independence because of an IPO or a different wealth event. To use the words of John Lennon[1], 'Life is what happens to you when you are busy making other plans'.

The previous chapter spoke about some meta-skills required to make FLAVOUR work at a point in time. But when we experience a significant change in our context, it often merits a slightly different set of approaches to move towards rediscovering our new FLAVOUR as we walk

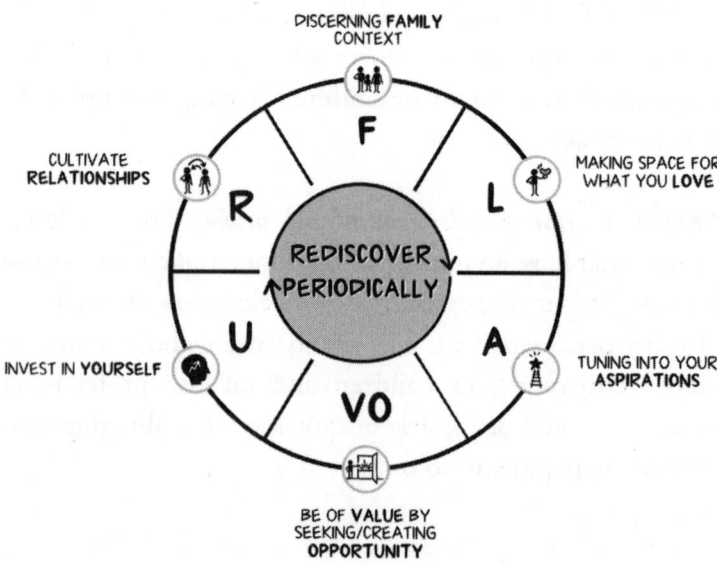

through life. We discuss a few approaches that might help you with the rediscovery!

## Get in Touch with Your Roots

Chapters 3, 4 and 5 speak about the inner work we all need to do as we go through our journey. While the criticality of self-awareness cannot be overstated as we go about our lives, its role during periods of key transitions becomes that much more critical as the stakes become higher. When I look back at my two years at IIM Ahmedabad about a quarter of a century earlier and reflect on which course had a big impact on me, it was a course called WAC (Written Analysis and Communication). It was not finance, marketing, operations or any other functional course. It was a course about how we make decisions and communicate our thought processes. We were given a case and we had to analyze it and spell out our recommendation in written form. The rigour we developed in analyzing still stays with me. For any case we were asked to follow 6 broad steps: 1) situational analysis, 2) problem definition, 3) generation of options, 4) criteria for decision, 5) evaluation of options and 6) decision. When we go through a transition, the criteria for decision making should emerge from our awareness around who we are and what we want. Tuning into that can make all the difference in the quality of life we end up leading. If I go back to the conversations I would have as a search consultant at Egon Zehnder, most candidates would jump from step 2 to step 5 without adequate generation of options and inner work on 'who they are' and 'what they really want'. Making decisions without adequate work in step 4 can get us deeper into the midlife mess that we might already be dealing with.

There is one element I would like to underscore in this exercise of self-awareness. It is about tuning into our early years. Sudhir Sitapati[2] (🎙) has an interesting insight into the context of how brands often rediscover their mojo and purpose. He speaks about how he likes to look at Brand Archeology to understand the birthing qualities of a brand. He mentions that very often brands end up drifting over time and the brand archaeology exercise can bring the focus back to what the brand is about. I find that when people are in phases of transition, they end up placing disproportionate emphasis on the last few years and that is a lost opportunity.

The journeys in Chapter 7 are a case in point. Soma's passion for painting could be traced back to her childhood. Sumeet's desire to transform education could be traced back to the impact his father had on him as a schoolteacher. Sucharita's desire to impact 'Bharat' could be traced to her brief immersion during IRMA. When I look back at the courses I really enjoyed at IIMA, they were the ones around organizational behavior. However, I kept telling myself that I ought to be enjoying math-based courses like quantitative methods, operations and financial derivatives. Pausing and reflecting on what has brought us joy at various points in our lives can provide us with directional cues, especially during phases of transition.

It turns out that our early years (first fifteen to twenty years) have more clues than we anticipate in giving us data around this question. Paradoxically enough, getting in touch with our roots gives us the wings to discover new possibilities.

This is also a time when we need to be mindful of the mental models around transitions that have shaped us from our early years that could actually become a limiting factor when we are trying to rediscover our FLAVOUR. One such mental model is that of looking for a trapeze to latch on to when we are in transition. But often, we might need to step into the unknown and take a leap of faith.

## Take a Leap of Faith

*Indiana Jones and the Last Crusade* starring Sean Connery and Harrison Ford is one of those movies I have watched many times over. I've lost count of how many times I've plunged into this movie, each viewing as fresh and captivating as the first. Bruce Feiler[3] (🎙), who has studied many life transitions, brought my attention to the interesting 'leap of faith' scene in the movie. In this scene,[4] Indiana Jones (played by Harrison Ford) faces a seemingly impassable chasm on his quest to find the Holy Grail. According to the ancient guidebook he carries, he must take a leap of faith from the lion's head to prove his worthiness. Standing at the edge and with no visible means to cross, Indiana struggles with doubt and fear. The chasm appears bottomless, and from his perspective, stepping forward would mean certain death. Yet, the urgency of his father's (played by Sean Connery) failing health and the quest's weight on his shoulders compel him to trust in something beyond logic and sight. In a moment of desperation and faith, Indiana closes his eyes and steps into the void. To his amazement, his foot lands on solid ground. It's revealed that a camouflaged bridge spans the chasm, painted to look exactly like the abyss below when viewed from the start of the leap.

As a student of transitions, the more I look around and look at people who are striving to play to their full potential, I see that they have often taken a leap of faith into the unknown letting go of something significant— most often either a relationship or a job that is offering comfort and predictability— Sumeet Mehta leaving P&G and exploring opportunities in education before joining Zee Learn; Sucharita Mukherjee leaving a cushy salary at Morgan Stanley in London before joining the start-up team at IFMR Holdings; Ravishankar leaving the comforts of his salary at Feedback Infra to focus on employability. This is not easy as for a large part of our life, we are used to grabbing the next trapeze before we let go of our current one. Herminia Ibarra[5] (🎤) uses the term 'liminality' to describe this 'in-between' phase—the equivalent of the chasm that needs to be crossed. It is a phase where we don't have the comfort of an identity that we can cling to. If someone asks the question 'what do you do?' at a gathering, we may not have a coherent answer. And that can be unnerving. However, therein lies the opportunity.

As a former search consultant and currently, as a transition adviser, I have seen this play out in the context of individuals having successful careers. The conversation is very often around whether they should take a career break/ sabbatical to figure out what next and the default tendency is not to do it because of the fear of the unknown. They keep trundling along either in a suboptimal role or grab the first one that comes their way through a search consultant rather than exploring what is possible I often nudge them pointing out that the upside in possibilities that they can discover due to this kind of a break because of higher mindspace and lesser sensitivity is much higher than the efficiency gains of clinging on to a trapeze and waiting for the next one to appear.

Another mental model that we grow up around is about taking decisions based on think first, do later kind of structure, where 'thinking things through' is prioritized. However, during transitions, sometimes taking action paves the way for new possibilities.

## Let Your Actions Guide Your Thinking

A lot of us are brought up with the paradigm of thinking before acting. A lot of our education reinforces this mental model as we approach life. All our exams during schooling and college life are often about what we think rather than what we do. Implicitly, unbeknownst to us, we assume that there is a unidirectional causality between thought and action.

When we try to rediscover our FLAVOUR at a point of inflection, I notice that we often hit a wall with our thinking. It is our actions that will help us break this logjam and move forward, especially in these situations. If I go back to the leap of faith in *Indiana Jones and the Last Crusade*, the bridge that appears when Indian Jones takes his first step is invisible to those who rely solely on their eyes. It can only be discovered by those who dare to believe and take that action of placing their foot forward.

When we experience a big transition (retirement, empty nesting, maternity, loss of a loved one), actions can help in the healing and solving for self-worth. Deepa Malik (🎙) is an Arjuna Award and Padma Shri winner and has won many international medals including a silver medal at the 2016 Rio di Janeiro Paralympics. She speaks about how her life was turned upside down when she was paralyzed waist down when she was around thirty because of a spinal tumor. She speaks about going through a phase where she was looking to be independent and wanted to prove to the world that she was not a liability. She started a small restaurant in Ahmednagar, spotting an opportunity to be of value to some young army officers who were looking for good food while employing several underprivileged kids. She discusses how she rebuilt her self-worth by doing this which led her to other pursuits like biking and swimming and eventually led her to compete at the highest level and bag medals in the Paralympic games on the global stage. She didn't start with a lofty purpose. She just told herself, given the context I am in, what is a baby step I can take which can move me in the right direction. This might be particularly relevant for homemakers during empty-nesting or professionals around retirement. That sudden loss of one big pillar can be disorienting.

The key is to craft a set of experiments based on what you believe your skills are, what energizes you and the family context and see how it plays out. It might be that the portfolio life is the answer that works for you. Or it might be that one of the elements of the portfolio grows and that becomes the 'one big thing' you grow into. In a lot of ways, this process is no different from how a venture capitalist invests in many companies without knowing which one would take off but if you construct the portfolio carefully, you know that something, somewhere will click!

I love a phrase that Herminia Ibarra[6] uses to describe the benefit of acting and iterating as compared to thinking and implementing. She says, 'When you are in a transition, you act your way into a new way of thinking. You don't think your way into a new way of acting.'

## Try to Follow Google's 20 per cent Rule in Your Life

Google's 20 per cent-time rule gained popularity when the firm went public in 2004.

In addition to their regular projects, its employees were encouraged to spend 20 per cent of their time working/ learning on topics they truly love, or were interested in. The company believed that this would make the employees

more creative and innovative. Many advances, including
AdSense and Google News, came from this initiative.

Several individuals have taken some variation of this
approach to their journeys, especially when they find that
there is a distinction between what they truly love (L) and
what they are working on that puts bread on the table
(VO). Given that there are commercial considerations,
they cannot drop what they are doing and plunge into their
passion. But they chip away for a long period before they
make a big pivot in that direction. These individuals play
the 20 per cent rule as a long game over many years and
pivot when the time is right.

Amish Tripathi (🎤) is an alumnus of IIM Calcutta
(batch of 1997). He nurtured his passion by writing on
mythology while pursuing his career in the financial services
world for fourteen years across companies like Standard
Chartered Bank, IDBI Bank, DBS Bank and IDBI Federal
Life Insurance. He states that given his family context,
he couldn't have pivoted earlier. It was only around 2011
when he wrote his second book, and the royalty revenues
of the book were significant, that he turned to full-time
writing. Till then, writing was the equivalent of a 20 per
cent project. Amish speaks about a period of seven to eight
years when he just prioritized three things: family, work
and writing to the exclusion of everything else before he
took the plunge to become a full-time writer.

In my journey, since 2016, my coaching and sounding
board advisory work has been paying the bills. The *Play to
Potential* podcast has been a 20 per cent project for me since

2017. Apart from playing a role in provoking reflection in thousands of people who have tuned into the content, it has also played the role of a 'trust building' function with some of the leaders who subsequently choose to work with me. It is also the seed that has led to the book that you now hold in your hand.

The 20 per cent rule, if applied strategically can potentially unlock new pathways and possibilities organically and can avoid sudden pauses and shifts that can be unnerving. 'Most people overestimate what they can do in one year and underestimate what they can do in ten years,' Bill Gates has said. This is specifically relevant in the context of how a sustained 20 per cent effort in a side project can compound and eventually possibly open up a new pathway.

## Choose Your Life Architecture Thoughtfully

Very often, when people are at a crossroads around a transition, the typical question they ask is 'what do I do now?' when they think of their talent-market fit (VO in FLAVOUR). Very often, there is a meta-question that requires deliberation that people often bypass, 'How do I want to architect my life?' There are many pathways to engaging in a certain topic. You could be an entrepreneur, employee, investor, part-time consultant, auditor, board member, volunteer, journalist or something else. Each of these has a different implication on time, money and some of the other elements of FLAVOUR.

When I look at how people frame their aspirations, I notice that they often fall into two broad categories:

1. Outside-in: There is a big problem out there and I need to take a shot at solving it.
2. Inside-out: This is the kind of person I want to be and I will see where it takes me.

Even if we look at the six journeys we profiled in Chapter 7, we can see the difference in the way they articulate their aspiration or angst about the status quo.

- **Ravi**: *To be respectful, be kind and be empathetic to others and enable others to become better storytellers.*
- **Sangeeta:** *Being responsible in the various roles she plays— daughter, wife, mother, teacher, volunteer.*
- **Soma:** *Juggle six balls efficiently: 1) children and husband, 2) painting, 3) work, 4) family and friends, 5) travel and 6) exercise and treks.*
- **Sucharita:** *Two billion people work in the informal sector globally and do not have access to affordable finance.*
- **Sumeet**: *270 million students are not going to grow up to their full potential.*
- **Vineet**: *Spread awareness about stories of 'real heroes' from India.*

Ravi, Sangeeta and Soma have their aspiration in a bit of an 'inside-out' language while Sumeet and Sucharita have an 'outside-in' frame. Vineet has a combination of both frames but has a greater tinge of inside-out. It is no coincidence that Ravi, Soma and Sangeeta have a portfolio life, Sucharita and Sumeet are building venture capital-funded enterprises at scale while Vineet is running his project like a movement!

Ashish Dhawan[7] (🎙), a leading philanthropist today, speaks about his transition after a successful run as a co-founder of ChrysCapital—a leading private equity fund that he ran from 1999 to 2012. At the height of his success, Ashish decided to walk away and start his journey in philanthropy. He recounts that he briefly toyed with the idea of being a professor and possibly creating additional material (like Sal Khan of Khan Academy) but mentions that Jay O. Light (dean of HBS at that time) dissuaded him from doing so because he felt Ashish would get bored with that choice. Ashish also mentions that at the time of the transition, he had been on a few boards and felt that he wanted to do something more proactive in system reform through a combination of grant-making, research, policy-making and working with the government to drive change. He felt he was an entrepreneur at heart and wanted to choose an architecture that enabled that!

Each one of us needs to be honest about the shape of our aspiration and strive to architect a life that is true to that aspiration.

## Be Fluid with Your Identities

When we experience a change of season, our choice about rediscovering our FLAVOUR is quite akin to a farmer's who, having finished a harvest cycle, has to choose which seeds to sow for the next season. The seed in question is our identity. How we relate to our identity and deal with it becomes a key element of unlocking possibilities.

Pramath Sinha[8](🎙), given the role he has played in establishing many educational institutes of repute like Ashoka University and Indian School of Business, has an interesting view on the link (or the lack of it) between educational qualification and careers. He mentions that the link between what we study and what our career turns out to be is becoming more and more tenuous by the day. I am exhibit A for this insight.

However, at every phase of transition, we tend to hold on to our past identity closely, whether it is our education (engineer, doctor, lawyer, journalist etc.) or our profession (consultant, investor, marketer, accountant). There is an evolutionary reason for that. Jennifer Garvey Berger[9] (🎙) states that thousands of years of evolution have led to our brain overestimating the changes that have happened to us to date but significantly underestimating the transformations that are ahead of us.

Just pause for a moment here. If you undertake time travel go back a decade or two and put yourself in the shoes of that version of you, do you think that person could have estimated where you would have come in terms of distance and direction? If I go back and asked my thirty-year-old self (who had just joined McKinsey in New Jersey) to lay out the various scenarios for me when I would be forty-five, none of them would have been anywhere close to where I am today. This gives me humility but also hope about what we all could become if we don't cling to our identities and get shackled by our past.

A related point here is that when we are going through a transition and rediscovering our FLAVOUR, it is critical to keep our identities small and have a healthy level of detachment from them. James Clear[10]($\bullet$) urges us to focus on the more enduring aspects of a particular identity that we can take with us into a new context. Instead of saying, 'I am a soldier,' you could say, 'I have a strong sense of discipline and have the back of people around me.' Instead of saying, 'I am an athlete,' you could say, 'I am the kind of person who trains my body hard and shows up every day for training.' In my case, rather than clinging on to terms like strategy consultant and headhunter, when I told myself that I am the kind of person that could build trusted relationships with senior leaders, I felt new possibilities open up.

A corollary to keeping our identities small is also for us to keep our ego in check when we are in transition. Very often, we might have climbed a mountain in a certain domain of our life but might be at the foothills of another climb. That might require us to have a certain level of humility and not judge the people around us in the emerging context. Atul Khatri[11] ($\bullet$) speaks about the phase when he was climbing the ladder of stand-up comedy while being the CEO of his IT hardware company. He mentions that a lot of his peers in the stand-up world were half his age and in a very different economic context. He says that he could not let that come in the way of how he engaged with them. The humility we show when we engage with some of these ecosystems especially at the foothills of a new climb, can make a big difference to how others engage with us and how the possibility takes shape.

You might notice that there might be a seeming contradiction of fluidity of identities with the section on getting in touch with our roots, which implies that some elements of who we are endure. I go back to the metaphor of the Ship of Theseus (that we discussed in Chapter 3) to reconcile the two. We are ever-evolving and when we take stock of who we are, there is likely to be a portion of us that has endured from our roots and some portions that are new and evolving. Being aware of this distinction is key as we march through life with awareness and intention.

## Be Curious, Stay Resilient, Engage and Connect the Dots

I was exposed to some of the nuances of the term potential when I was a leadership adviser at Egon Zehnder. My role was to help clients find leaders for their organizations in the context of a business requirement. As we would evaluate candidates, we would often look at three levels of capability in an individual.

*Level 1—Demonstrated Performance*: This refers to 'what' has the individual done in his or her career to date. This refers to the functional capability that somebody has developed, the industry knowledge that they have accumulated, the roles they have done and the education they have had. This was the CV view. The kind of things we would put on a CV with details about various jobs, titles, and accomplishments. At the first level, one could clearly see what value that person would add on day 1 to a role.

*Level 2—Competency:* This was typically the next level of assessment and often the plane around which we would make most of our assessments. The primary lens was the 'how'. How does a leader get things done? How do they drive results and strategy? How do they set a vision? How do they lead the teams? How do they influence their peers? How do they develop systems and processes? One could say this view encapsulated the person's leadership style and provided commentary on the muscles that had already been built that could be deployed in a certain context.

*Level 3—Potential:* This assessment was one level deeper and focused on who the people were 'being', rather than just how they were doing things. This view didn't quite comment on the current capability but involved us taking a punt on the long-term with the individual. We focused on four elements that we felt captured elements of potential.[12] Brief simplified descriptions below:

a. *Being Curious:* Openness to learning, trying new things and to feedback
b. *Being Engaging:* Relating to people and building meaningful human connections
c. *Being Resilient:* Grinding through the mundane and bouncing back from shocks

d. *Being Insightful:* Connecting the dots across various domains and systems thinking

The distinction between Level 2 and Level 3 is that Level 2 is about action that you take deliberately while Level 3 is about natural inclination and about what energizes you. The weight we would give to Levels 1, 2 and 3 would depend on the nature of the opportunity. If it was a stable, mature context, we would over-index on Level 1. But if it was a sunrise industry in a cutting-edge domain subject to the features of VUCA (volatile, uncertain, complex, ambiguous) or BANI (brittle, anxious, non-linear, incomprehensible), we would over-index on Level 3.

When we are rediscovering our FLAVOUR, in a lot of ways it is about bringing out all the elements of Level 3 to the fore. It is about experimenting and being curious about learning new things and about being aware of how we are feeling as we go through the experiments. As Ravishankar Iyer says, it is useful to adopt the mindset of a scientist, frame a few hypotheses as we move forward and either validate or reject them based on our experiences. A lot of exploring new ecosystems will come through having conversations with people and engaging with them. Not every experiment will be successful. Things take time to evolve and gain traction. That requires resilience for us to keep walking. Finally, a big chunk of rediscovering FLAVOUR is staying aware and tuning into what is emerging in front of us, how we are feeling and then being able to connect the dots and 'making sense' of the data. That ability to distil insight from data for ourselves can help in fine-tuning our path. When we are in a transition and trying to rediscover our FLAVOUR, who we are being ends up mattering as much or more than what we are doing.

## Seek Green Shoots but Cut Losses if Required

When we transition contexts and are rediscovering our FLAVOUR, we need to rethink how we measure progress. Traditional measures of outcomes (revenue, title, cash flow etc.) break down because the chances are we are at the foothills of a new compounding curve that needs time and patience.

Whitney Johnson[13]($\quad$) leverages principles of disruptive innovation as espoused by the late Clay Christiansen and applies that to people's journeys. She urges us to see our life as a series of S curves[14]. When we move from one S curve to another, she says that we change our actions but we often do not change the report card with which we measure ourselves. Unless that evolves to reflect our emerging aspirations across our various identities, we are likely to end up disappointing ourselves in the process.

James Clear[15]($\quad$) uses the example of melting ice to drive home the point about metrics. What works in phase transition happens to apply in life transition! He says that if we heat a block of ice from $-10^0$ Celsius to $-1^0$ Celsius, we don't quite see any change on the outside but that is not to say that work is not being done. It is just that the change is not visible. This reminds me of a quote from Jacob Riis—

that is displayed on the walls of San Antonio Spurs—the legendary NBA Basketball team: 'When nothing seems to help, I go and look at a stonecutter hammering away at his rock perhaps a hundred times without as much as a crack showing in it. Yet at the hundred and first blow, it will split in two, and I know it was not that blow that did it, but all that had gone before.' When we are in transition, we never know which is that hundred and first blow where we will see traction. We sometimes have to just keep ploughing through.

When I started the *Play to Potential* podcast in 2016, each episode would hardly get a few hundred clicks. I would compare myself to some of the other content creators on YouTube who would be receiving thousands and millions of clicks. Slowly, I tried to divert my attention to some of the qualitative metrics (gratitude from people who are in transition and see value in an episode, 100 loyal fans rather than a million clicks, and speaking engagements based on the podcast quality) and that has kept me going and has eventually resulted in this very book.

Having said that, we might come across situations where we feel we have taken a turn that we shouldn't have. We must reflect and cut losses rather than keep climbing the wrong tree. It is a fine balance between persistence and knowing when to quit. Nandan Nilekani (🎤) is a case in point. After a successful stint as the architect of the Aadhaar project (as a Rajya Sabha member), Nandan mentioned he was keen to earn his seat on the table (so that his ideas could be taken with adequate weight and importance) and wanted to compete in Lok Sabha elections. However, as he competed in the elections, he discovered that it was a B2C endeavour and not in line with his distinctiveness. 'My effectiveness comes from being what I am good at, which is a technology-led transformation agent and in using my talents and abilities to solve large intractable problems and make that available to anybody who wants to use it,' he recounted as he spoke about moving away from politics to come back to being a tech evangelist and a transformation agent in the various roles he plays. The key is to keep reflecting on the experience to see if we should keep persisting or cut our losses.

Rediscovering our FLAVOUR when we go through a transition is not about following a predictable pathway from A to B. It is about leaning into the unknown, crafting some experiments thoughtfully, proactively listening to how the initiatives are shaping up, and how we feel about them, crafting metrics that are fit for your purpose that helps us measure to see how we are doing in this phase, and then either doubling down or cutting losses and moving forward.

The key is for us to realize that life keeps flowing. It does not stay static. We keep evolving from moment to moment. What works for us at a certain point in time may not work in another phase of life. The best we can do is to stay closely tuned to the emerging context and the emerging version of who we are and be intentional about rediscovering our FLAVOUR as we go through this rollercoaster called life.

As we go through the seasons of our lives, we must pay as much attention to the transition as we pay to the season itself. It is also critical that we learn both sets of skills that have been outlined in Chapter 8 and this chapter. One set of skills (in Chapter 8) will help you thrive in a season. The set of skills in this chapter will help you rediscover your FLAVOUR as you move to a different season of your life.

# Contextual Audio Snippets from the Podcast

- **Audio Clip 9.01:** Sudhir Sitapati on getting in touch with our roots
- **Audio Clip 9.02:** Bruce Feiler on leap of faith
- **Audio Clip 9.03:** Herminia Ibarra on liminality
- **Audio Clip 9.04:** Herminia Ibarra on acting your way into a new way of thinking
- **Audio Clip 9.05:** Deepa Malik on starting a restaurant after being paralyzed
- **Audio Clip 9.06:** Amish Tripathi and the 20 per cent project
- **Audio Clip 9.07:** Ashish Dhawan on choices post ChrysCapital
- **Audio Clip 9.08:** Pramath Sinha on the tenuous link between education and careers
- **Audio Clip 9.09:** Jennifer Garvey Berger on overestimating past changes and underestimating future transformations

- **Audio Clip 9.10:** James Clear on keeping our identity small
- **Audio Clip 9.11:** Atul Khatri on being fluid with different ecosystems
- **Audio Clip 9.12:** Nandan Nilekani on cutting losses

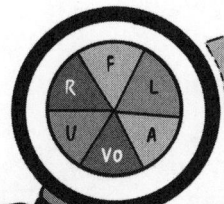

# REDISCOVERING *our* FLAVOUR

## GET IN TOUCH WITH YOUR ROOTS

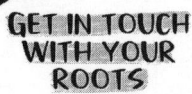

Inner work of tuning into what gives us joy and our aspirations can open up pathways for the future

## TAKE A LEAP OF FAITH

Take the leap and let go of the past.

There is risk but therein lies the OPPORTUNITY

## LET YOUR ACTIONS GUIDE YOUR THINKING

Act and then reflect.

Avoid getting into the zone of 'analysis paralysis'

## FOLLOW 20 PERCENT RULE

Bake a passion or initiative on the side on 20 percent time till it is prudent to take the plunge

## CHOOSE YOUR LIFE ARCHITECTURE THOUGHTFULLY

Focus on meta-decision during transitions: What is the shape of what we want to do?

## BE FLUID WITH YOUR IDENTITIES

Attachment to our identities can hinder discovering new possibilities.

Keep identities small and be open to engage with the new

## BE CURIOUS, STAY RESILIENT, ENGAGE AND CONNECT THE DOTS

Curiosity opens new pathways, but requires resilience, engaging with people and connecting the dots

## SEEK GREENSHOOTS BUT CUT LOSSES IF REQUIRED

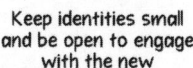

Wait for the uplift of compounding curve, but watch out for signals that tell us that we are climbing the wrong tree

# Parting Thoughts

Very often when we think of the word high potential, stalwarts like Sachin Tendulkar, Serena Williams, P.V. Sindhu, Viswanathan Anand, Steve Jobs, A.R. Rahman, Amitabh Bachchan, Lata Mangeshkar and so on come to our mind. We naturally drift to people who are at the top of their field. I used to have a similar view on potential as well. However, as I started getting more curious about potential, I started noticing that all of us were dealt with a different set of cards. While the distribution of opportunity is possibly skewed, I truly believe that the distribution of potential is quite uniform across the population. The real question, I believe, is whether we are playing the game to the best of our capability, given the cards life has dealt us. Like the late Thurgood Marshall said, are we doing what we can with what we have? And are we multi-dimensional in the way we think about our potential? I hope this book has given you some food for thought and action in finding a holistic response to that question.

I have wondered if we should make a distinction between individuals who are leading a well-rounded life and those who are playing to full potential. I notice that people often see leading a well-rounded life as some sort of a compromise/settlement/cop out. I believe that if we are true to our multi-dimensional aspiration and proactively reconcile the tensions between the various domains of our lives, we can strive to play to our full potential while leading a well-rounded life. When we invest in some of the other domains (like L, U and R) it can impact the quality of the value we add to the world (VO) and hence, the impact we have over the long run. I am not sure if there is a dichotomy there. I see leading a full life more as a flywheel that can put us on the path of playing to our full potential as a human being.

I also notice that the language around potential is often designed to laud the hunter more than the gatherer, the striker more than the goalkeeper or the earner more than the homemaker. I hope that the language in this book gives agency to people playing varying roles in the family to play to their respective potential.

I should also be explicit about where I stand when it comes to my relationship with Ikigai. I have found the language helpful in my journey and in the context of some of the choices I have made. However, just like how a vision statement doesn't translate to a strategic plan, I feel that Ikigai is too high-level to inform some of the 'on the ground' choices we have to make in our lives. To go back to the quote from Lincoln, we could use Ikigai to get a sense of where we need to eventually head and FLAVOUR to navigate the swamps, deserts and chasms that we encounter. It doesn't have to be an either/or.

For a long time in my life, I understood language as a descriptive tool. Something we use to illustrate what is going on around us. Of late, I have come to believe that language is more of a generative tool. The language we use can shape the future we build for ourselves. I sincerely hope that the various themes illustrated in the book and the FLAVOUR framework provide you the language to explore new possibilities and architect a life that puts you on the path of playing to your full potential.

# Ten Podcast Conversations to Go Deeper

I have tried to sprinkle the relevant excerpts from the *Play to Potential* podcast at various points in the book to embellish a particular point I make. In addition, I would also like to call your attention to the following ten long-form conversations at the podcast (links to Apple and Spotify in the additional resources section) if you wish to go deeper into some of the topics discussed in the book.

1. **Dr Tasha Eurich** on *Insight*
   *Topics*: Self-awareness unicorns, the distinction between internal and external self-awareness, limitations of introspection and mindfulness beyond meditation

2.  **Ravi Venkatesan** on *What the Heck Do I Do with My Life*
    *Topics*: Future of work and how we could stay relevant, being intentional about life, tuning into different forms of capital and how we should measure our life

3.  **Prof. Lynda Gratton** on *The 100-year Life*
    *Topics*: Moving from a three-stage life (study, work, retire) to a multi-stage one, tangible vs intangible assets and choosing the intensity of work

4.  **Prof. Stew Friedman** on *Total Leadership*
    *Topics*: Driving harmony across four domains—self, work, home and community, managing and influencing stakeholder expectations and role of authenticity, integrity and creativity

5.  **Prof. Dan Cable** on *Exceptional*
    *Topics*: Building your own personal highlights reel, feedback as a big bang vs drip feed, engaging different parts of our brain to think creatively about our future

6.  **Lloyd Reeb** on *From Success to Significance*
    *Topics*: Being a chief life officer, measuring what matters, moving from interest to identity, keeping a low centre of gravity, maintaining a margin in life and pausing after success

7.  **Prof. Herminia Ibarra** on *Working Identity*
    *Topics*: Acting your way into new thinking, pausing to reinvent, experimenting with different pathways, perils of foreclosure and transitioning from well-paying, time greedy careers

8.  **Bruce Feiler** on *Life Is in the Transitions*
    *Topics*: Disruptors and life-quakes, shape-shifting instead of resilience, three phases of a transition, taking a leap of faith and making sense of scars instead of wounds

9.  **Prof. Ashley Whillans** on *Time Smart*
    *Topics*: Understanding time poverty, knowing when money stops moving the needle, optimizing vs satisficing and changing our relationship with time

10. **Ayse Birsel** on *Design Your Life*
    *Topics*: Life design vs product design, the power of metaphors, getting playful about life design, deconstruction and reconstruction and what we can learn from Nelson Mandela

    However, if you are looking for curated short-form nuggets from the speakers above on some of the sub-themes, you can find them in the Members section of the podcast at www.playtopotential.com.

# Acknowledgements

I have come to realize that it takes a village to get a book out. There are many people to thank without whom this book would not have been possible.

At the outset, I want to honour my father, S. Jayaraman, who passed away in 2008 after a courageous seven-month battle with colon cancer. His passing was a pivotal event in my life, leading me to a path of self-discovery and setting me on the path that culminated in the creation of this book.

I would like to thank Rajiv Lochan for prompting me to write a book and Prakash Iyer for making it real and introducing me to Radhika Marwah, my commissioning editor at Penguin Random House India. Thank you to her and the Penguin team, including Yash Daiv, Aakriti Khurana, Aishvarya Misra, Prateek Agarwal and Vijesh Kumar, for supporting and cheerleading me as I went through this lonely process for the first time.

Sincere thanks to my friend and sounding board on this writing journey, Shweta Mani. Like most things, I realize that writing is a skill that needs to be honed over many years. Working with her has clarified and shaped a lot of my thinking around the book and helped me communicate the ideas in a more reader-friendly manner.

Thank you to my illustrator Tanmay Vora who has the uncanny ability to distil pages of complex information into a pithy visual that captures the essence. A picture is worth a thousand words, they say. With Tanmay, I would say it is worth at least around 5000 words. His chapter summaries captures the many nuances of a 5000-word chapter in one visual.

When I began writing this book, it started out as a 'string of pearls' where I was trying to curate the wisdom I have gleaned from the *Play to Potential* podcast and my experiences. My friend and former colleague at Egon Zehnder, Vivek Khemka, provoked me to think bigger and pushed me to see if I wanted to say something original and put out a 'recipe' that ties things together. While I didn't have it on day one of writing the book, it slowly emerged as I marinated in the topic over a few months. I am grateful for his provocation.

Special thanks to Venkatesh (Venky) Srinivasan for sharing the quote from Abraham Lincoln (I share it at the beginning of Chapter 2) when I was sparring with him. As I mention in the 'Parting Thoughts' section, this quote has provided much greater clarity and conviction around what I am trying to say and how it reconciles with ikigai, a concept that a lot of people are familiar with.

This book would be incomplete without the 6 journeys that have been profiled in Chapter 7. At the risk of over-doing it, let us say that they help bring FLAVOUR to (life in) the book. In the process, they have been candid, vulnerable and generous with their time. Thank you to Ravishankar Iyer, Sangeeta Shahaney, Soma Biswas Vajpayee, Sucharita Mukherjee, Sumeet Mehta and Vineet Panchhi.

Thank you to Akash Deore and Arman Bansod for their help in curating some of the audio/video content that embellish the book. That required many hours of painstaking work. Thank you also to Pinaaz Patrawala for patiently helping coordinate with the many guests at the podcast to ensure that their thoughts are being represented appropriately in the book. This book stands on the shoulders of the wisdom from some of these giants.

Several people have been generous with their time and attention in reviewing the various versions of the book and giving their valuable perspectives: Bama Balakrishnan, Dr Cyrus Vakil, Gayatri Yadav, Harish Bhat, Janani Kannan, Moomal Mehta, Mrinalini Mirchandani, Samardeep Subandh, Sucharita Narasimhan, Vikas Srivastava, Sudhir Sitapati and Venkatesh Srinivasan. Their suggestions and provocations have helped me shape the book in many ways.

Last but not the least, thanks to my family—my mother Brindha Jayaraman, my parents-in-law Brigadier (Retd) V. Mahalingam and Saraswathi Mahalingam, my wife Kamini and our children—Pragya and Nirmal, who encouraged me and sparred with me along the way and put up with my 'cave mode' while I was writing this book.

# Additional Resources

# Notes

## Introduction

1   Podcast website www.playtopotential.com; also available on Spotify, Apple Podcasts and other platforms.

2   Several guests on the *Play to Potential* podcast are on the Thinkers 50 List—considered the Oscars for Management Thinking.

## 1. The Midlife Conundrum

1   Abraham Maslow was an American psychologist who in 1943 proposed that there is a hierarchy of needs and humans keep going up the pyramid as the needs are met. The order from lowest to highest are—Physiological, Safety, Love and Belonging, Esteem and Self-Actualization.

2   Author of *If You Are So Smart, Why Aren't You Happy?*, India, Portfolio, 2016.

3   Each time you see this microphone sign, it is an indication that we have a curated audio clip from this speaker extracted from

the *Play to Potential* podcast. Please see end of chapter for more detail.

4   You might notice that the three numbers do not add up to 100. The balance 6 per cent, apparently, is accounted for by the few people who might be stuck in stages 1 or 2 or some that might be in some transition between stages.

## 2.  Limitations of Ikigai

1   As portrayed in the movie *Lincoln* (2012), directed and produced by Steven Spielberg.
2   The documentary *Blue Zones* on Netflix by Dan Buettner covers pura vida, ikigai and a few other related concepts.
3   Partly driven by the book *Ikigai: The Japanese Secret to a Long and Happy Life* authored by Francesc Miralles and Hector Garcia that was published in 2016.
4   My video, 'Why using Ikigai as a framework' that I recorded in 2016: https://bit.ly/DJMyWhy2016.
5   Blue Ocean is a term used in the book *Blue Ocean Strategy* written by Renee Mauborgne and W. Chan Kim. Blue Oceans are new spaces which are low on competition while Red Oceans are spaces where there is cutthroat competition.
6   Professor at London Business School and co-author of *The 100-Year Life* with Andrew Scott (Bloomsbury, 2016).

## 3.  What Lies Beneath

1   Author of the book *Paradox of Choice*.
2   Author of *Insight: Why We're Not as Self-Aware as We Think, and How Seeing Ourselves Clearly Can Help Us Succeed at Work and in Life* (Currency, 2017).
3   This question is inspired by the work of Prof. Stew Friedman of Wharton; he is the author of *Total Leadership* (Harvard Business Review, 2008).

4   Rich Fernandez was a guest at the *Play to Potential* podcast and headed (at the time of the podcast) Search Inside Yourself Leadership Institute, a leadership development organization incubated in Google.

5   https://tim.blog/2019/02/20/the-tim-ferriss-show-transcripts-jim-collins-361/

## 4. How 360 and 365 Is Your 360

1   While the exact origin of this phrase is unknown, it is often attributed to Ken Blanchard, author and leadership thinker.

2   I recognize that I might be carrying biases given what I do for a living. Do apply appropriate discount rates to account for my leanings as you read the next few paragraphs.

3   In the epic Ramayana, Hanuman is a Hindu God—half-monkey and half-human—who is a devoted follower of Prince Ram.

4   American academic and businessman, known for his work on disruptive innovation and author of the book *How Will You Measure Your Life?*

5   I must mention that I only speak to some of the personal connections like spouse, sibling(s), parent(s) and friends if the individual is comfortable with it.

## 5. Tuning into Our Values and Principles

1   'A Simple Way to Make Better Decisions' by Amanda Reill published in *Harvard Business Review*, 5 December 2023.

2   https://www.jnj.com/our-credo

3   We discuss coherence in the context of the framework outlined in the next chapter.

4   The curation by nuggets and themes is available at www.playtopotential.com.

5   Author of *The Power of Regret: How Looking Backward Moves Us Forward* (Riverhead Books, 2022).

6   I am grateful to Vijay Sarathi (friend and dorm-mate at IIMA) for nudging me to see this!
7   Am grateful to Kuldeep Jain, a friend and a senior leader in McKinsey India at that time who leaned in to make this possible.
8   Loosely translated to 'intellect of a shrewd businessman coupled with fearless audacity'.
9   Excerpt from the IIT Delhi yearbook published around the Silver Jubilee Reunion for the batch of 1997.
10  Ramesh Srinivasan is a senior partner at McKinsey, New York and co-author of the book *The Journey of Leadership*.

## 6.   Crafting a FLAVOUR-ful Life

1   Professor at Wharton Business School at University of Pennsylvania and author of *Total Leadership Harvard Business School Pr* (2008).
2   Amish Tripathi is the author of many books around mythology including the Shiva trilogy and the Ram Chandra series. His books have sold seven million copies and been translated into twenty Indian and international languages since 2010.
3   https://www.ted.com/talks/dan_pink_the_puzzle_of_motivation?language=en
4   https://www.instagram.com/paperinkandmore/
5   Author of *Beginners: The Curious Power of Lifelong Learning*
6   Social Venture Partners is a group of philanthropists trying to make a difference. Learn more about them at: https://svpindia.org./
7   Professor at London Business School and author of *The 100-Year Life*.
8   Robert J. Waldinger is an American psychiatrist, psychoanalyst and Zen priest. He is a part-time professor of psychiatry at Harvard Medical School and directs the Harvard Study of Adult Development.
9   Professor at London Business School and author of *Working Identity* (Harvard Business Review Press, 2004).

10  Name changed for reasons of confidentiality.
11  A phrase often used by Arthur Brooks in his book *From Strength to Strength: Finding Success, Happiness and Deep Purpose in the Second Half of Your Life* (Portfolio, 2022).
12  Author of *Design the Life You Love: A Step-by-Step Guide to Building a Meaningful Future* (Ten Speed Press; Illustrated edition, 2015).

## 7.  Some FLAVOUR-ful Lives

1  If one had to be technically correct, there are more than eight billion unique lives on the planet. For the purposes of the LEGO House, it is safe to assume that the number of cumulative visitors to the house would be much lower than 915 million.
2  We also have detailed video interviews with these individuals if you want to go deeper into any of the stories. Links are provided at the end of the chapter.
3  Scholastic Aptitude Test (SAT) is a multiple-choice computer-based test that is often used in the context of college admissions in some countries.
4  A Chinese game similar to the card game rummy, but one that is played with 144 tiles.
5  Read the LinkedIn article here: https://www.linkedin.com/pulse/bhag-scary-baby-steps-soma-biswas-vajpayee/?trackingId=11v52RbvQ7aGu%2FU3Gb6gbg%3D%3D
6  Matt Langdon, *The Hero Handbook,* the United Kingdom, Magination Press, 27 January 2021.

## 8. Meta-Skills for a FLAVOUR-ful Life

1  Reference to Frank Sinatra and his song 'My way'.
2  According to the research of Tim Spector, professor of genetic epidemiology, King's College, London; he is also a specialist in studies of twins.

3    I came across this approach in my conversations with friend/ mentor, Rajiv Lochan (who adapted this approach from McKinsey's Engagement Leadership Workshop [ELW] Programme).

4    Lloyd Reeb helped launch the Halftime Institute, a global team that teaches, coaches and connects successful men and women in pursuit of significance. He is the author of the book *From Success to Significance.*

5    A term I learnt from Navin Wadhwani, head of investment banking at JP Morgan India.

6    It happens to be that phase of life where people around my age have to reconcile with the fact that we need bifocals to see clearly.

7    Volpert Family Associate Professor of Business Administration at Harvard Business School and author of *Time Smart: How to Reclaim Your Time and Live a Happier Life* (Harvard Business Review Press, 2020).

8    Raj is the author of *If You Are So Smart, Why Aren't You Happy?* (Portfolio, 2016).

## 9.  Rediscovering our FLAVOUR of the season

1    The words feature in the song 'Beautiful boy (Darling Boy)' by John Lennon.

2    Author of *The CEO Factory: Management Lessons from Hindustan Unilever* (Juggernaut, 2019).

3    Author of *Life Is in the Transitions* (Penguin Press, 2020).

4    Scene available on YouTube.

5    Professor at London Business School and author of *Working Identity* (Harvard Business Review, 2004).

6    Herminia Ibarra, *Act Like a Leader, Think Like a Leader* (Harvard Business Press, 2015).

7    Founder-CEO of The Convergence Foundation, founder-chairperson of Central Square Foundation and founder-trustee of Ashoka University.

8    Chairperson of Ashoka University (as of March 2024) and author of *Learn, Don't Study: A Guide for Students and Parents to Succeed in the Ever-Changing Landscape of the Modern Workplace* (Penguin Business, 2023).

9    Jennifer Garvey Berger is the author of *Unlocking Leadership Mindtraps: How to Thrive in Complexity* (Stanford University Press, 2019).

10   Author of *Atomic Habits* (Avery, 2018).

11   Popular stand-up comedian.

12   Claudio Fernandez Araoz, a former consultant at Egon Zehnder, captures the framework well in his *HBR* article published in June 2014 titled, '21st Century Talent Spotting'.

13   Author of *Disrupt Yourself: Master Relentless Change and Speed Up Your Learning Curve* (Harvard Business Review, 2019).

14   'S curve' is a term used to describe the shape of the curve that represents the growth and adoption of technologies, products or processes. While it is applicable in the context of disruptive innovation, it is also often applicable in the context of personal reinvention.

15   Author of *Atomic Habits*.